C-3826 CAREER EXAMINATION SERIES

This is your
PASSBOOK for...

Phlebotomist

Test Preparation Study Guide
Questions & Answers

COPYRIGHT NOTICE

This book is SOLELY intended for, is sold ONLY to, and its use is RESTRICTED to individual, bona fide applicants or candidates who qualify by virtue of having seriously filed applications for appropriate license, certificate, professional and/or promotional advancement, higher school matriculation, scholarship, or other legitimate requirements of education and/or governmental authorities.

This book is NOT intended for use, class instruction, tutoring, training, duplication, copying, reprinting, excerption, or adaptation, etc., by:

1) Other publishers
2) Proprietors and/or Instructors of "Coaching" and/or Preparatory Courses
3) Personnel and/or Training Divisions of commercial, industrial, and governmental organizations
4) Schools, colleges, or universities and/or their departments and staffs, including teachers and other personnel
5) Testing Agencies or Bureaus
6) Study groups which seek by the purchase of a single volume to copy and/or duplicate and/or adapt this material for use by the group as a whole without having purchased individual volumes for each of the members of the group
7) Et al.

Such persons would be in violation of appropriate Federal and State statutes.

PROVISION OF LICENSING AGREEMENTS – Recognized educational, commercial, industrial, and governmental institutions and organizations, and others legitimately engaged in educational pursuits, including training, testing, and measurement activities, may address request for a licensing agreement to the copyright owners, who will determine whether, and under what conditions, including fees and charges, the materials in this book may be used them. In other words, a licensing facility exists for the legitimate use of the material in this book on other than an individual basis. However, it is asseverated and affirmed here that the material in this book CANNOT be used without the receipt of the express permission of such a licensing agreement from the Publishers. Inquiries re licensing should be addressed to the company, attention rights and permissions department.

All rights reserved, including the right of reproduction in whole or in part, in any form or by any means, electronic or mechanical, including photocopying, recording, or by any information storage and retrieval system, without permission in writing from the Publisher.

Copyright © 2025 by
National Learning Corporation

212 Michael Drive, Syosset, NY 11791
(516) 921-8888 • www.passbooks.com
E-mail: info@passbooks.com

PASSBOOK® SERIES

THE *PASSBOOK® SERIES* has been created to prepare applicants and candidates for the ultimate academic battlefield – the examination room.

At some time in our lives, each and every one of us may be required to take an examination – for validation, matriculation, admission, qualification, registration, certification, or licensure.

Based on the assumption that every applicant or candidate has met the basic formal educational standards, has taken the required number of courses, and read the necessary texts, the *PASSBOOK® SERIES* furnishes the one special preparation which may assure passing with confidence, instead of failing with insecurity. Examination questions – together with answers – are furnished as the basic vehicle for study so that the mysteries of the examination and its compounding difficulties may be eliminated or diminished by a sure method.

This book is meant to help you pass your examination provided that you qualify and are serious in your objective.

The entire field is reviewed through the huge store of content information which is succinctly presented through a provocative and challenging approach – the question-and-answer method.

A climate of success is established by furnishing the correct answers at the end of each test.

You soon learn to recognize types of questions, forms of questions, and patterns of questioning. You may even begin to anticipate expected outcomes.

You perceive that many questions are repeated or adapted so that you can gain acute insights, which may enable you to score many sure points.

You learn how to confront new questions, or types of questions, and to attack them confidently and work out the correct answers.

You note objectives and emphases, and recognize pitfalls and dangers, so that you may make positive educational adjustments.

Moreover, you are kept fully informed in relation to new concepts, methods, practices, and directions in the field.

You discover that you are actually taking the examination all the time: you are preparing for the examination by "taking" an examination, not by reading extraneous and/or supererogatory textbooks.

In short, this PASSBOOK®, used directedly, should be an important factor in helping you to pass your test.

PHLEBOTOMIST

DUTIES
A medical technical position specializing in letting blood, blood circulation, clots, etc. Examines patients, diagnoses conditions, makes treatment recommendations, and removes blood. Performs related duties.

SUBJECT OF EXAMINATION
The written test will be designed to test for knowledge, skills, and/or abilities in such areas as:
1. Principles and practices of phlebotomy;
2. Blood circulation principles, practices and terminology; and
3. Laboratory and diagnostic equipment and procedures.

CLINICAL LABORATORY SERVICES

CAREER DESCRIPTIONS

CONTENTS

	Page
I. Certified Laboratory Assistant	1
II. Clinical Chemist	2
III. Cytotechnologist	3
IV. Histologic Technician	4
V. Medical Laboratory Technician	5
VI. Medical Technologist	6
VII. Specialist in Blood Bank Technology	9

CLINICAL LABORATORY SERVICES

CAREER DESCRIPTIONS

Physicians utilize a number of tests and devices Which make a general appraisal of a patient's condition—taking the patient's pulse, temperature, and blood pressure; listening to the heart and lungs with a stethoscope; looking into the nasal passages with a nasoscope; or into the eyes with an ophthalmoscope. With these instruments, the physician can detect gross changes in the functioning of the various organs, and, in most common illnesses, make a diagnosis.

But there are many illnesses whose symptoms are not so easily detectable. These are illnesses in which there are changes in the body fluids and tissues not noticeable by observation. They include chemical changes in the blood, urine, lymph; increases or decreases in the count of various types of white or red blood cells; microscopic changes in the structure of the cells of a diseased tissue or organ; and the presence of parasites, viruses, or bacteria in the blood or diseased tissue.

To detect these, physicians must send specimens of blood, urine, or tissue for a variety of highly technical tests performed in the laboratory. Combining laboratory findings with other observations, they are then able to make an accurate diagnosis.

Laboratory examination of body fluids and tissues serves other purposes as well. Blood tests must be made to determine blood types when a blood transfusion is needed. There are certain blood types which if combined in conception, produce abnormal offspring, and these types can be detected by laboratory tests. Some individuals have violent allergic reactions to different kinds of medications, and laboratory tests are used to detect this type of sensitivity.

Although physicians need the results of these tests for evaluation and diagnosis, they do not conduct the tests themselves. Instead, these tests are made by clinical laboratory personnel. These specialists provide laboratory services ranging from routine tests to highly complex analyses, and their skill and education levels differ significantly. In the following pages, several specialties in clinical laboratory services are discussed in detail to point out the variety of career choices available in this area of work.

I. Certified Laboratory Assistant

The certified laboratory assistant performs a variety of routine tests and procedures under the direct supervision of a medical technologist or physician. The certified laboratory assistant works in all areas—bacteriology, chemistry, hematology, parasitology, serology, blood banking, and urinalysis. Special tasks performed include collecting blood specimens, grouping and typing blood, preparing and staining slides for microorganisms, analyzing body fluids for chemical components, and examining urine, blood, and body fluids with the microscope. In large laboratories, the assistant may concentrate in one area of work such as the preparation of blood smears in hematology. In addition to performing routine tests, assistants may store and label plasma; clean and sterilize laboratory equipment, glassware, and instruments; prepare solutions following standard laboratory formulas and procedures; keep records of tests; and label specimens.

Most laboratory assistants work in hospitals; however, some work in independent laboratories, physicians' offices, clinics, public health agencies, pharmaceutical firms, and research institutions. These places are often located in large cities and populous States.

Medical laboratory assistants generally work a 40-hour week and, in hospitals, some night and weekend duty can be expected. Assistants usually work closely with medical technologists, pathologists, and other laboratory personnel. Laboratories are generally well-lighted and clean. Although unpleasant odors and specimens of many kinds of diseased tissue often are present, few hazards exist if proper methods of sterilizing and handling specimens, materials, and equipment are used.

Job Requirements

The certified laboratory assistant (CLA) program is accredited by the Committee on Allied Health Education and Accreditation of the American Medical Association. Accuracy, dependability, and the ability to work under pressure are necessary characteristics for persons considering this career. In addition, manual dexterity and normal color vision are desirable. Graduation from an accredited high school, preferably with an ability and interest in science and mathematics, or a certificate of equivalency is required for admission to an accredited school. The 12-month course of practical and technical education includes classroom instruction plus laboratory training. CLA schools are
primarily in hospitals, although in some areas they are located in technical schools, community colleges, and on military bases. Graduates who pass the American Society of Clinical Pathologists (ASCP) Board of Registry examination may use the letters CLA (ASCP) after their names which indicates that they are certified laboratory assistants.

Opportunities

Hospitals and other facilities throughout the country are expected to continue to need competently trained laboratory assistants to meet demands for laboratory services and to free medical technologists and medical laboratory technicians for the more complex, highly technical procedures. Employment of laboratory assistants is expected to decrease in urban areas and increase in rural areas. The number of persons seeking to enter the field of laboratory assistants is expected to exceed the number of openings from growth and replacement needs. Consequently, persons seeking jobs in this field may face competition for positions of their choice. A certified laboratory assistant may advance to the medical laboratory technician level by acquiring an associate degree from an accredited institution.

II. Clinical Chemist

Clinical chemists use chemical tests, procedures, techniques, and equipment of varying complexity to obtain information used in the diagnosis and treatment of disease. They perform, or direct other laboratory personnel who perform, chemical tests on blood, serum, urine, spinal fluid, and other body materials to gather clinical data. Clinical chemists detect abnormalities in the amount of proteins, hormones, enzymes, and other constituents in the body. They also are concerned with the analytical and research aspects of disease states, toxic substances and drugs, including metabolism and effects on body functions at the tissue and organ levels. Clinical chemists are responsible for insuring that their test results have a high degree of reliability, since many of these data are utilized by physicians as part of any clinical assessment of a patient.

Teaching and training persons in clinical chemistry can be part of clinical chemists' responsibilities, and they may engage in administrative or managerial activities in such positions as supervisor or laboratory director.

The majority of clinical chemist works in private or hospital laboratories, while the remainder work in private industry, Government agencies, and educational institutions.

Job Requirements
Persons considering this career must have such qualities as analytical ability and the capability of working precisely, both independently and as part of a team.

The educational minimum for a limited number of entry positions in this field is a bachelor's degree in chemistry or biochemistry. However, the majority of clinical chemists has a master's, Ph.D., or M.D. degree and finds substantially greater employment opportunities. The National Registry in Clinical Chemistry, through an examination, certifies clinical chemists with a doctoral, master's, or bachelor's degree who meet specified qualifications. Those who qualify receive the designation of clinical chemist (CC) or clinical chemistry technologist (CCT).

The American Board of Clinical Chemistry (ABCC), through an examination process, certifies clinical chemists who have a doctoral degree plus substantial experience in the field. They issue those who qualify the designation of diplomat (DABCC).

The American Society of Clinical Pathologists (ASCP) also certifies clinical chemists who meet specified requirements and issues the designation of Spec C (ASCP).

Opportunities
Job opportunities for clinical chemists with advanced degrees are expected to be favorable during the next decade. Qualified clinical chemists can advance to supervisory or administrative positions, enter research or teaching activities, or become proprietors of clinical laboratories. Advancement in the field is generally governed by experience, work expertise, and continued studies at higher levels.

III. Cytotechnologist

The cytotechnologist is a trained laboratory technologist who works under the direction of a pathologist. The prime responsibility of the cytotechnologist is to detect cell changes caused by different disease processes. These specialists prepare cell samples, obtained from various body areas, for examination by using special staining techniques which make the specimens more visible. Smears of the cell samples are then placed on slides, inserted under a microscope, and examined by the cytotechnologist. Cytotechnologists are trained to recognize minute abnormalities in the color, size, and shape of cell substances, and, in many cases, their findings are the first warning signs of cancer. As a result, physicians are able to diagnose and treat cancer long before discovering its existence by alternate methods. In addition, cytotechnologists also use a variety of methods to detect abnormal hormone conditions.

Most cytotechnologists work in a hospital, clinic, or private laboratory. Laboratories are usually well lighted and clean. Specimens of different kinds of diseased tissues and unpleasant odors are often present, but few hazards exist because of safety procedures employed in laboratories.

Job Requirements
The minimum education preparation for this career includes graduation from high school or its equivalent plus 2 years of college with 12 semester hours in science, at least 8 of which must be in biological science. An individual who is a certified medical technologist MT (ASCP), or has a bachelor's degree in science from an accredited college or university may also be eligible for admission to this program. This is followed by a 12-month cytotechnology course accredited by the Committee on Allied Health Education and Accreditation of the American Medical Association. The course consists of classroom study and practical laboratory experience dealing

with normal and abnormal cell variations in body systems. The education program is conducted under the close supervision of experienced cytopathologists and cytotechnologists. Upon successful completion of this 12-month formal study, the student is eligible for the certifying examination given by the Board of Registry of the American Society of Clinical Pathologists. Those who pass may use the designation CT (ASCP) after their names. The National Certifying Agency for Medical Laboratory Personnel will also administer a certifying examination, and the individual who passes this examination will be designated by the letters CLSp-CT. Many States have licensing requirements for cytotechnologists, and the appropriate agency should be contacted to determine exact legal standards.

Opportunities

The employment outlook for cytotechnologists is favorable, with the demand for trained workers exceeding the supply at this time. This trend is expected to continue but many jobseekers may have to choose work locations outside of large urban areas, where competition for available openings is considerable. Cytotechnologists can advance to supervisory positions, move into research activities, or become teachers in their fields. In any case, advancement is based on experience, skill level, and the completion of the advanced education courses.

IV. Histologic Technician

The histologic technician, using specialized or routine methods, prepares sections of body tissue for microscopic examination by a pathologist. This includes specimens of human and animal tissues used for' diagnosis, research, or instruction. The histologic technician prepares portions of body tissues selected for examination; freezes and cuts tissue samples, mounts them on slides, and stains them with special dyes so that specific structural details or substances will be visible under the microscope. Often while the team in surgery waits, it is the histologic technician who prepares the tiny sections of the patient's body tissue for the microscope examination that will determine whether body malfunction or malignancy are present. The histological technician must perform these procedures using good skills, knowledge, and judgment.

With the recent advances in technology, histologic technicians are specializing in techniques involving the use of the electron microscope or special studies which help determine a patient's diagnosis. Histologic technicians may also work with a wide variety of sophisticated instruments which are manually operated or semi-automated.

Most histologic technicians work in hospital laboratories and are required, at times, to work shifts and weekends. The working conditions in laboratories are generally good, with clean, well-lighted surroundings. Specimens of different types of diseased tissue and unpleasant odors are usually present; however, few hazards exist because of the safety procedures employed in modern laboratories.

Job Requirements

Persons considering this career should be interested in the physical, chemical, and biological sciences and be able to perform work in a precise, dependable, and responsible way. In addition, manual dexterity and normal color vision are essential. The basic educational preparation for this career includes graduation from high school or the equivalent, plus the completion of a 1-year course accredited by the American Medical Association Committee on Allied Health Education and Accreditation. Programs are usually given in a hospital or laboratory facility. Some of the subject areas studied in this program include histochemistry, anatomy, histology, laboratory mathematics, microscopy, processing techniques, preparation of specimens, medical terminology, and chemistry.

After completing the training program, the graduate can receive certification from several different agencies. The National Certifying Agency for Medical Laboratory Personnel will administer an examination for the histologic technician. The individuals who pass the examination will be certified and allowed to use the initials CLSp-HT after their names. A graduate may also receive certification from the Board of Registry of the American Society of Clinical Pathologists by passing an examination given by the Registry. Individuals who pass this exam are then allowed to use the initials HT(ASCP) after their names.

Opportunities

Since physicians are making wider use of laboratory tests in the diagnosis and treatment of diseases, many new jobs should develop in the future. In addition, population growth, greater health consciousness, and expansion of prepayment programs for medical care that make it easier for people to pay for services and affecting the growth of jobs in this field. Qualified histologic technicians can advance to supervisory positions or, after further education and special training, move into research or teaching activities. The level to which a technician rises, of course, is governed by experience, skill development, and completion of advanced education courses.

V. Medical Laboratory Technician

Medical laboratory technicians are mid-level laboratory workers who function under the supervision of a medical technologist or laboratory supervisor. They perform a wide range of tests and laboratory procedures which are more complex than the routine duties assigned to laboratory assistants but which do not require the technical knowledge and management skills of highly trained medical technologists.

Medical laboratory technicians are qualified by education and experience to perform clinical laboratory testing which requires minimal exercise of independent judgment. Working under appropriate supervision, they perform a number of laboratory tests in chemistry, hematology, urinalysis, blood banking, serology, and microbiology. These test results are used to develop the information needed by physicians in determining the presence, cause, and extent of diseases in patients. As part of their work, medical technicians often use laboratory instruments ranging from microscopes to highly computerized instruments such as the automated blood analyzers which analyze blood and body fluids for chemical constituents such as cholesterol, sugar level, and hemoglobin content.

Most medical laboratory technicians work in hospitals, while others work in independent laboratories, physicians' offices, clinics, public health agencies, pharmaceutical firms, and research institutions. Medical laboratory technicians generally work a 40-hour week, and in hospitals some night and weekend duty can be expected. Technicians usually work closely with medical technologists, pathologists, laboratory assistants, and other medical personnel. Laboratories generally are well-lighted and clean. Although unpleasant odors and specimens of many kinds of diseased tissue often are present, few hazards exist if proper methods of sterilization and handling of specimens, materials, and equipment are used.

Job Requirements

Accuracy, dependability, the ability to follow directions, and the ability to work .under pressure are important personal characteristics for a laboratory technician. In addition, manual dexterity and normal color vision are highly desirable. Preparation for a career as a medical laboratory technician requires a high school education followed by an associate degree from an accredited junior or community college and then clinical experience in an approved laboratory. The AMA's Committee on Allied Health, Education an Accreditation approves programs for the medical laboratory technician. After completing the course work in clinical education, the graduate can receive certification from several different agencies. The National Certifying Agency for Medical Laboratory Personnel administers an examination for the clinical laboratory technician. The individuals who pass this examination are certified and allowed to use the initials CLT after their name. Graduates may also receive certification from the Board of Registry of the American Society of Clinical Pathologists by passing an examination given by the Registry. Individuals who pass this examination are then allowed to use the initials MLT (ASCP) after their names. They may also receive registration with the American Medical Technologists. This registration can be acquired by high school graduates who have completed a 2-year school program approved by the Accrediting Bureau of Medical Laboratory Schools. The American Medical Technologists will also register medical laboratory technician students who have completed a 50-week Armed Forces course in medical laboratory techniques together with approved laboratory experience.

Opportunities

Hospitals and other facilities are expected to continue to need competently trained medical laboratory technicians to meet increased demands for laboratory services and to free medical technologists and other laboratory staff for the more complex, highly technical procedures and supervisory duties.

Employment of laboratory technicians is expected to expand faster than the average for all occupations through the mid-2020's, as physicians make wider use of laboratory tests in routine physical checkups and in the diagnosis and treatment of diseases. Also affecting the growth in the field are population increase, greater public health consciousness, and expansion of prepayment programs for medical care that make it easier for people to pay for services. The number of persons seeking to enter the field of medical laboratory technician is expected to exceed the number of openings resulting from growth and replacement needs. Consequently, persons seeking jobs in this field may face competition for positions of their choice. A medical laboratory technician may advance to medical technologist or a supervisory position by acquiring the necessary education and experience. The technician position provides a new intermediate level on the laboratory career ladder thus opening the way for individuals to move more easily to higher levels. Colleges are being encouraged to provide for the upward mobility of students who are seeking to insure transferability of credits earned toward their B.S. degrees.

VI. Medical Technologist

Medical technologists are highly skilled generalist laboratory scientists who perform chemical, microscopic, microbiological, hematological, serological, and radiobioassay tests which require the exercise of independent judgment and responsibility in the diagnosis and treatment of diseases. They must be able to relate the results of the laboratory tests to the normal healthy state and to the presence of diseases or other conditions which may alter test results. Medical technologists assure the validity of test results by using statistical measures of precision and accuracy and other methods of quality control. The medical technologist may also introduce methods and new equipment into the laboratory.

Medical technologists identify, count, and note any irregularities in the size, shape, and other characteristics of red and white blood cells and compare the results with previous tests using

microscopes and modern electronic equipment. They also test blood for over 200 chemical substances including the sugar content, hemoglobin content, cholesterol level, and the presence of other substances which are altered in diseases such as hemophilia, anemia, leukemia, heart condition, and mononucleosis. Technologists examine urine for its acid, sugar, and protein content, and use microscopes to detect evidence of blood cells and other foreign substances which could indicate the presence of such diseases as diabetes, nephritis, or bladder cancer. Medical technologists also collect blood from donors, type the blood, and cross match it for compatibility with the blood of patients who need tranfusions. They grow cultures of bacteria and fungi from patients' blood, sputum, feces, or discharge from a sore or wound; identify the organism; and determine which antibiotics are most effective in each case. Technologists perform other tests to search for and identify parasites living in the patient's body and determine what antibodies and other disease-fighting elements are present in the patient's blood.

Technologists are trained to operate special apparatus and a wide array of precision instruments - electronic cell counters, automatic chemical analyzers, chromatographs, centrifuges, microscopes, and computers. They also operate complex electronic equipment to measure the amount and location of radioactivity in the analysis of hormones and other substances. Some medical technologists perform all of the tasks described while others specialize in one particular area. For example, clinical chemistry technologists are those who specialize in determining the presence and quantity of chemical substances in the blood and other body fluids. Hematology technologists concentrate their efforts on performing tests for clotting factors and studying slides of blood cells to facilitate the diagnosis of illnesses. Another example of specialization in this work is the microbiology technologist. These specialists are concerned primarily with growing, isolating, and identifying the bacteria, fungi, and other organisms present in the human body. Some technologists, especially those in larger hospitals or clinics, also teach medical technology students, laboratory assistants, medical students, and pathology residents. Most administrative and supervisory duties in the laboratory are performed by medical technologists.

About two-thirds of all medical technologists work in hospital laboratories. Other employers are clinics; physicians in private practice; pharmaceutical, reagent, and instrument manufacturers; insurance companies; medical, dental, and veterinary colleges; city, State and Federal health agencies; and research organizations for cancer, tuberculosis, and other diseases. In general, medical technologists work five 8-hour days a week. Those employed by hospitals, where emergency duty is often required, may be on call for evening duties. Others may work the night shift or have weekend work as part of their regular schedule. Clinical laboratories, particularly in hospitals, are open 24 hours a day, 7 days a week. While medical technology does present the occupational hazard of infection from bacteria or viruses, such illness rarely occurs.

Job Requirements
Persons considering a career in medical technology should have an aptitude for chemistry, physics, and biology; should like working in a laboratory; and have the ability to do careful, reliable work under pressure. Medical technologists should be skilled at using their hands, since they work with small instruments and delicate equipment. Communication and human relation skills are also important since they help them to function as supervisors and educators.

Other assets are good health, normal vision, and an ability to distinguish fine shades of color. Some materials handled by technologists might seem unpleasant to those who lack scientific interests in education, but medical technologists cannot afford to be unduly squeamish.

The education requirements for certification as a medical technologist include 3 years of college plus 1 year of clinical education in a school of medical technology approved by the

Committee on Allied Health Education and Accreditation of the American Medical Association. Educational requirements are designed to result in a bachelor's degree.

The pre-professional part of the college program includes a minimum of 16 semester hours each in approved chemistry and biological science courses. Also a minimum of one semester of college-level mathematics and basic microbiology. Some programs also require physics, genetics, medical chemistry, and computer technology.

At the end of 3 years (or 90 semester hours), students are ready to begin the clinical-education phase in one of the approved schools of medical-technology located in hospitals or university health and medical centers. Some universities with a School of Allied Health Professions of a school of Allied Health Sciences integrate the entire 4-year curriculum to provide clinical laboratory experience simultaneously with basic science courses. Most medical technology programs accept a limited number of students (15 or less); therefore, application for admissions should be made at the end of the fifth semester of college. A few of the hospital schools require a college degree before admission.

After completing college work and the clinical education in an approved school of medical technology, the graduate can receive certification from several different agencies. The National Certifying Agency for Medical Laboratory Personnel administers an examination for clinical laboratory scientists. Individuals who pass this examination are certified and allowed to use the initials CLS after their names. The graduate may also receive certification from the Board of Registry of the American Society of Clinical Pathologists by passing an examination given by the Registry. Individuals who pass this examination are then allowed to use the initials MT (ASCP) after their names. Specialty examinations are also given by both agencies in chemistry, microbiology, hematology, and blood banking, so that a technologist is eligible for these occupational areas after special additional instruction or experiences are obtained in the particular field. The American Medical Technologists (AMT) grants registration and certification to those who have completed 90 semester hours in an accredited college with specific course requirements, have completed 1 year of laboratory experience, and have passed their certification examinations. American Medical Technologists have developed a career ladder to enable technicians qualified to apply for the medical technologist's certification examination after completion of 3 years of approved laboratory experience. AMT-registered medical technologists use the designation MT after their names.

Opportunities

Medical technology has experienced one of the fastest growth rates in the health field in the past decade. Employment prospects are expected to continue to be good during the next decade because of the greater number of people who require laboratory tests every day, increased dependence on laboratory tests for routine care as well as diagnosis and treatment, and the broadening coverage of government-sponsored and private health insurance plans.

Opportunities for advancement in this field are good for qualified medical technologists. Promotions are usually based on experience, work expertise, and knowledge obtained through acquisition of master's degrees, advanced education courses, and seminars and workshops sponsored by various professional societies.

VII. Specialist in Blood Bank Technology

Specialists in blood bank (SBB) technology perform routine and specialized tests in blood bank immunohematology. They develop their skills and expertise through advanced training in such areas as donor selecting; drawing blood; blood typing, preparing, and storing; compatibility and antibody studies; transfusion reactions; investigation of hemolytic diseases of the newborn, and quality control. Some specialists in blood bank technology concentrate their efforts in one particular area such as research associated with a laboratory, university, or government-related facility. Specialists in blood banking sometimes work as supervisors, educators, technical consultants and function as part of the health team, providing essential health services to patients.

Specialists in blood bank technology work in many types of facilities including community blood centers, private hospital blood banks; university affiliated blood banks, independent laboratories, Red Cross blood centers and may also be part of a university faculty. Specialists work as an integral part of the laboratory and health-care team in providing direct support for patient care. This work may require some weekend and night duty, including emergency calls. Generally, there are no specific physical requirements for successful job performance except good health and good psychomotor skills.

Job Requirements

Individuals considering this career must complete a 1-year education program in blood bank technology which is accredited by the American Medical Association (AMA), Committee on Allied Health Education and Accreditation (CAHEA), and the Committee on Education of the American Association of Blood Banks (AABB). In order to qualify for admission to an accredited education program, candidates must be either certified as medical technologist, MT (ASCP), or have a bachelor's degree in a biological or physical science, plus at least 1 year of acceptable clinical laboratory experience.

Most SBB education programs are conducted in hospital or community blood banks and consist of classroom activities combined with practical work in the blood bank.

The American Association of Blood Banks (AABB) and the American Society of Clinical Pathologists (ASCP) administer a certification examination for those who qualify. Individuals who pass the certification examination are permitted to use the designation SBB (ASCP) after their names. The National Certifying Agency for Medical Laboratory Personnel will administer an examination for specialists in blood bank technology, and the individual who passes this examination will be granted the designation CLSp-BB.

Opportunities

The employment outlook for specialists in blood bank technology is favorable, and currently the demand exceeds the supply. Qualified specialists may advance to supervisory or administrative positions, or move into teaching or research activities. The criteria for advancement in this field are experience, technical expertise, and completion of advanced education courses.

HOW TO TAKE A TEST

I. YOU MUST PASS AN EXAMINATION

A. WHAT EVERY CANDIDATE SHOULD KNOW

Examination applicants often ask us for help in preparing for the written test. What can I study in advance? What kinds of questions will be asked? How will the test be given? How will the papers be graded?

As an applicant for a civil service examination, you may be wondering about some of these things. Our purpose here is to suggest effective methods of advance study and to describe civil service examinations.

Your chances for success on this examination can be increased if you know how to prepare. Those "pre-examination jitters" can be reduced if you know what to expect. You can even experience an adventure in good citizenship if you know why civil service exams are given.

B. WHY ARE CIVIL SERVICE EXAMINATIONS GIVEN?

Civil service examinations are important to you in two ways. As a citizen, you want public jobs filled by employees who know how to do their work. As a job seeker, you want a fair chance to compete for that job on an equal footing with other candidates. The best-known means of accomplishing this two-fold goal is the competitive examination.

Exams are widely publicized throughout the nation. They may be administered for jobs in federal, state, city, municipal, town or village governments or agencies.

Any citizen may apply, with some limitations, such as the age or residence of applicants. Your experience and education may be reviewed to see whether you meet the requirements for the particular examination. When these requirements exist, they are reasonable and applied consistently to all applicants. Thus, a competitive examination may cause you some uneasiness now, but it is your privilege and safeguard.

C. HOW ARE CIVIL SERVICE EXAMS DEVELOPED?

Examinations are carefully written by trained technicians who are specialists in the field known as "psychological measurement," in consultation with recognized authorities in the field of work that the test will cover. These experts recommend the subject matter areas or skills to be tested; only those knowledges or skills important to your success on the job are included. The most reliable books and source materials available are used as references. Together, the experts and technicians judge the difficulty level of the questions.

Test technicians know how to phrase questions so that the problem is clearly stated. Their ethics do not permit "trick" or "catch" questions. Questions may have been tried out on sample groups, or subjected to statistical analysis, to determine their usefulness.

Written tests are often used in combination with performance tests, ratings of training and experience, and oral interviews. All of these measures combine to form the best-known means of finding the right person for the right job.

II. HOW TO PASS THE WRITTEN TEST

A. NATURE OF THE EXAMINATION

To prepare intelligently for civil service examinations, you should know how they differ from school examinations you have taken. In school you were assigned certain definite pages to read or subjects to cover. The examination questions were quite detailed and usually emphasized memory. Civil service exams, on the other hand, try to discover your present ability to perform the duties of a position, plus your potentiality to learn these duties. In other words, a civil service exam attempts to predict how successful you will be. Questions cover such a broad area that they cannot be as minute and detailed as school exam questions.

In the public service similar kinds of work, or positions, are grouped together in one "class." This process is known as *position-classification*. All the positions in a class are paid according to the salary range for that class. One class title covers all of these positions, and they are all tested by the same examination.

B. FOUR BASIC STEPS

1) Study the announcement

How, then, can you know what subjects to study? Our best answer is: "Learn as much as possible about the class of positions for which you've applied." The exam will test the knowledge, skills and abilities needed to do the work.

Your most valuable source of information about the position you want is the official exam announcement. This announcement lists the training and experience qualifications. Check these standards and apply only if you come reasonably close to meeting them.

The brief description of the position in the examination announcement offers some clues to the subjects which will be tested. Think about the job itself. Review the duties in your mind. Can you perform them, or are there some in which you are rusty? Fill in the blank spots in your preparation.

Many jurisdictions preview the written test in the exam announcement by including a section called "Knowledge and Abilities Required," "Scope of the Examination," or some similar heading. Here you will find out specifically what fields will be tested.

2) Review your own background

Once you learn in general what the position is all about, and what you need to know to do the work, ask yourself which subjects you already know fairly well and which need improvement. You may wonder whether to concentrate on improving your strong areas or on building some background in your fields of weakness. When the announcement has specified "some knowledge" or "considerable knowledge," or has used adjectives like "beginning principles of..." or "advanced ... methods," you can get a clue as to the number and difficulty of questions to be asked in any given field. More questions, and hence broader coverage, would be included for those subjects which are more important in the work. Now weigh your strengths and weaknesses against the job requirements and prepare accordingly.

3) Determine the level of the position

Another way to tell how intensively you should prepare is to understand the level of the job for which you are applying. Is it the entering level? In other words, is this the position in which beginners in a field of work are hired? Or is it an intermediate or advanced level? Sometimes this is indicated by such words as "Junior" or "Senior" in the class title. Other jurisdictions use Roman numerals to designate the level – Clerk I, Clerk II, for example. The word "Supervisor" sometimes appears in the title. If the level is not indicated by the title, check the description of duties. Will you be working under very close supervision, or will you have responsibility for independent decisions in this work?

4) Choose appropriate study materials

Now that you know the subjects to be examined and the relative amount of each subject to be covered, you can choose suitable study materials. For beginning level jobs, or even advanced ones, if you have a pronounced weakness in some aspect of your training, read a modern, standard textbook in that field. Be sure it is up to date and has general coverage. Such books are normally available at your library, and the librarian will be glad to help you locate one. For entry-level positions, questions of appropriate difficulty are chosen – neither highly advanced questions, nor those too simple. Such questions require careful thought but not advanced training.

If the position for which you are applying is technical or advanced, you will read more advanced, specialized material. If you are already familiar with the basic principles of your field, elementary textbooks would waste your time. Concentrate on advanced textbooks and technical periodicals. Think through the concepts and review difficult problems in your field.

These are all general sources. You can get more ideas on your own initiative, following these leads. For example, training manuals and publications of the government agency which employs workers in your field can be useful, particularly for technical and professional positions. A letter or visit to the government department involved may result in more specific study suggestions, and certainly will provide you with a more definite idea of the exact nature of the position you are seeking.

III. KINDS OF TESTS

Tests are used for purposes other than measuring knowledge and ability to perform specified duties. For some positions, it is equally important to test ability to make adjustments to new situations or to profit from training. In others, basic mental abilities not dependent on information are essential. Questions which test these things may not appear as pertinent to the duties of the position as those which test for knowledge and information. Yet they are often highly important parts of a fair examination. For very general questions, it is almost impossible to help you direct your study efforts. What we can do is to point out some of the more common of these general abilities needed in public service positions and describe some typical questions.

1) General information

Broad, general information has been found useful for predicting job success in some kinds of work. This is tested in a variety of ways, from vocabulary lists to questions about current events. Basic background in some field of work, such as sociology or economics, may be sampled in a group of questions. Often these are principles which have become familiar to most persons through exposure rather than through formal training. It is difficult to advise you how to study for these questions; being alert to the world around you is our best suggestion.

2) Verbal ability

An example of an ability needed in many positions is verbal or language ability. Verbal ability is, in brief, the ability to use and understand words. Vocabulary and grammar tests are typical measures of this ability. Reading comprehension or paragraph interpretation questions are common in many kinds of civil service tests. You are given a paragraph of written material and asked to find its central meaning.

3) Numerical ability

Number skills can be tested by the familiar arithmetic problem, by checking paired lists of numbers to see which are alike and which are different, or by interpreting charts and graphs. In the latter test, a graph may be printed in the test booklet which you are asked to use as the basis for answering questions.

4) Observation

A popular test for law-enforcement positions is the observation test. A picture is shown to you for several minutes, then taken away. Questions about the picture test your ability to observe both details and larger elements.

5) Following directions

In many positions in the public service, the employee must be able to carry out written instructions dependably and accurately. You may be given a chart with several columns, each column listing a variety of information. The questions require you to carry out directions involving the information given in the chart.

6) Skills and aptitudes

Performance tests effectively measure some manual skills and aptitudes. When the skill is one in which you are trained, such as typing or shorthand, you can practice. These tests are often very much like those given in business school or high school courses. For many of the other skills and aptitudes, however, no short-time preparation can be made. Skills and abilities natural to you or that you have developed throughout your lifetime are being tested.

Many of the general questions just described provide all the data needed to answer the questions and ask you to use your reasoning ability to find the answers. Your best preparation for these tests, as well as for tests of facts and ideas, is to be at your physical and mental best. You, no doubt, have your own methods of getting into an exam-taking mood and keeping "in shape." The next section lists some ideas on this subject.

IV. KINDS OF QUESTIONS

Only rarely is the "essay" question, which you answer in narrative form, used in civil service tests. Civil service tests are usually of the short-answer type. Full instructions for answering these questions will be given to you at the examination. But in case this is your first experience with short-answer questions and separate answer sheets, here is what you need to know:

1) **Multiple-choice Questions**

Most popular of the short-answer questions is the "multiple choice" or "best answer" question. It can be used, for example, to test for factual knowledge, ability to solve problems or judgment in meeting situations found at work.

A multiple-choice question is normally one of three types—
- It can begin with an incomplete statement followed by several possible endings. You are to find the one ending which *best* completes the statement, although some of the others may not be entirely wrong.
- It can also be a complete statement in the form of a question which is answered by choosing one of the statements listed.

- It can be in the form of a problem – again you select the best answer.

Here is an example of a multiple-choice question with a discussion which should give you some clues as to the method for choosing the right answer:

When an employee has a complaint about his assignment, the action which will *best* help him overcome his difficulty is to
  A. discuss his difficulty with his coworkers
  B. take the problem to the head of the organization
  C. take the problem to the person who gave him the assignment
  D. say nothing to anyone about his complaint

In answering this question, you should study each of the choices to find which is best. Consider choice "A" – Certainly an employee may discuss his complaint with fellow employees, but no change or improvement can result, and the complaint remains unresolved. Choice "B" is a poor choice since the head of the organization probably does not know what assignment you have been given, and taking your problem to him is known as "going over the head" of the supervisor. The supervisor, or person who made the assignment, is the person who can clarify it or correct any injustice. Choice "C" is, therefore, correct. To say nothing, as in choice "D," is unwise. Supervisors have and interest in knowing the problems employees are facing, and the employee is seeking a solution to his problem.

2) True/False Questions

The "true/false" or "right/wrong" form of question is sometimes used. Here a complete statement is given. Your job is to decide whether the statement is right or wrong.

SAMPLE: A roaming cell-phone call to a nearby city costs less than a non-roaming call to a distant city.

This statement is wrong, or false, since roaming calls are more expensive.

This is not a complete list of all possible question forms, although most of the others are variations of these common types. You will always get complete directions for answering questions. Be sure you understand *how* to mark your answers – ask questions until you do.

V. RECORDING YOUR ANSWERS

Computer terminals are used more and more today for many different kinds of exams.

For an examination with very few applicants, you may be told to record your answers in the test booklet itself. Separate answer sheets are much more common. If this separate answer sheet is to be scored by machine – and this is often the case – it is highly important that you mark your answers correctly in order to get credit.

An electronic scoring machine is often used in civil service offices because of the speed with which papers can be scored. Machine-scored answer sheets must be marked with a pencil, which will be given to you. This pencil has a high graphite content which responds to the electronic scoring machine. As a matter of fact, stray dots may register as answers, so do not let your pencil rest on the answer sheet while you are pondering the correct answer. Also, if your pencil lead breaks or is otherwise defective, ask for another.

Since the answer sheet will be dropped in a slot in the scoring machine, be careful not to bend the corners or get the paper crumpled.

The answer sheet normally has five vertical columns of numbers, with 30 numbers to a column. These numbers correspond to the question numbers in your test booklet. After each number, going across the page are four or five pairs of dotted lines. These short dotted lines have small letters or numbers above them. The first two pairs may also have a "T" or "F" above the letters. This indicates that the first two pairs only are to be used if the questions are of the true-false type. If the questions are multiple choice, disregard the "T" and "F" and pay attention only to the small letters or numbers.

Answer your questions in the manner of the sample that follows:

32. The largest city in the United States is
    A. Washington, D.C.
    B. New York City
    C. Chicago
    D. Detroit
    E. San Francisco

1) Choose the answer you think is best. (New York City is the largest, so "B" is correct.)
2) Find the row of dotted lines numbered the same as the question you are answering. (Find row number 32)
3) Find the pair of dotted lines corresponding to the answer. (Find the pair of lines under the mark "B.")
4) Make a solid black mark between the dotted lines.

VI. BEFORE THE TEST

Common sense will help you find procedures to follow to get ready for an examination. Too many of us, however, overlook these sensible measures. Indeed, nervousness and fatigue have been found to be the most serious reasons why applicants fail to do their best on civil service tests. Here is a list of reminders:

- Begin your preparation early – Don't wait until the last minute to go scurrying around for books and materials or to find out what the position is all about.
- Prepare continuously – An hour a night for a week is better than an all-night cram session. This has been definitely established. What is more, a night a week for a month will return better dividends than crowding your study into a shorter period of time.
- Locate the place of the exam – You have been sent a notice telling you when and where to report for the examination. If the location is in a different town or otherwise unfamiliar to you, it would be well to inquire the best route and learn something about the building.
- Relax the night before the test – Allow your mind to rest. Do not study at all that night. Plan some mild recreation or diversion; then go to bed early and get a good night's sleep.
- Get up early enough to make a leisurely trip to the place for the test – This way unforeseen events, traffic snarls, unfamiliar buildings, etc. will not upset you.
- Dress comfortably – A written test is not a fashion show. You will be known by number and not by name, so wear something comfortable.

- Leave excess paraphernalia at home – Shopping bags and odd bundles will get in your way. You need bring only the items mentioned in the official notice you received; usually everything you need is provided. Do not bring reference books to the exam. They will only confuse those last minutes and be taken away from you when in the test room.
- Arrive somewhat ahead of time – If because of transportation schedules you must get there very early, bring a newspaper or magazine to take your mind off yourself while waiting.
- Locate the examination room – When you have found the proper room, you will be directed to the seat or part of the room where you will sit. Sometimes you are given a sheet of instructions to read while you are waiting. Do not fill out any forms until you are told to do so; just read them and be prepared.
- Relax and prepare to listen to the instructions
- If you have any physical problem that may keep you from doing your best, be sure to tell the test administrator. If you are sick or in poor health, you really cannot do your best on the exam. You can come back and take the test some other time.

VII. AT THE TEST

The day of the test is here and you have the test booklet in your hand. The temptation to get going is very strong. Caution! There is more to success than knowing the right answers. You must know how to identify your papers and understand variations in the type of short-answer question used in this particular examination. Follow these suggestions for maximum results from your efforts:

1) Cooperate with the monitor

The test administrator has a duty to create a situation in which you can be as much at ease as possible. He will give instructions, tell you when to begin, check to see that you are marking your answer sheet correctly, and so on. He is not there to guard you, although he will see that your competitors do not take unfair advantage. He wants to help you do your best.

2) Listen to all instructions

Don't jump the gun! Wait until you understand all directions. In most civil service tests you get more time than you need to answer the questions. So don't be in a hurry. Read each word of instructions until you clearly understand the meaning. Study the examples, listen to all announcements and follow directions. Ask questions if you do not understand what to do.

3) Identify your papers

Civil service exams are usually identified by number only. You will be assigned a number; you must not put your name on your test papers. Be sure to copy your number correctly. Since more than one exam may be given, copy your exact examination title.

4) Plan your time

Unless you are told that a test is a "speed" or "rate of work" test, speed itself is usually not important. Time enough to answer all the questions will be provided, but this does not mean that you have all day. An overall time limit has been set. Divide the total time (in minutes) by the number of questions to determine the approximate time you have for each question.

5) Do not linger over difficult questions

If you come across a difficult question, mark it with a paper clip (useful to have along) and come back to it when you have been through the booklet. One caution if you do this – be sure to skip a number on your answer sheet as well. Check often to be sure that you have not lost your place and that you are marking in the row numbered the same as the question you are answering.

6) Read the questions

Be sure you know what the question asks! Many capable people are unsuccessful because they failed to *read* the questions correctly.

7) Answer all questions

Unless you have been instructed that a penalty will be deducted for incorrect answers, it is better to guess than to omit a question.

8) Speed tests

It is often better NOT to guess on speed tests. It has been found that on timed tests people are tempted to spend the last few seconds before time is called in marking answers at random – without even reading them – in the hope of picking up a few extra points. To discourage this practice, the instructions may warn you that your score will be "corrected" for guessing. That is, a penalty will be applied. The incorrect answers will be deducted from the correct ones, or some other penalty formula will be used.

9) Review your answers

If you finish before time is called, go back to the questions you guessed or omitted to give them further thought. Review other answers if you have time.

10) Return your test materials

If you are ready to leave before others have finished or time is called, take ALL your materials to the monitor and leave quietly. Never take any test material with you. The monitor can discover whose papers are not complete, and taking a test booklet may be grounds for disqualification.

VIII. EXAMINATION TECHNIQUES

1) Read the general instructions carefully. These are usually printed on the first page of the exam booklet. As a rule, these instructions refer to the timing of the examination; the fact that you should not start work until the signal and must stop work at a signal, etc. If there are any *special* instructions, such as a choice of questions to be answered, make sure that you note this instruction carefully.

2) When you are ready to start work on the examination, that is as soon as the signal has been given, read the instructions to each question booklet, underline any key words or phrases, such as *least, best, outline, describe* and the like. In this way you will tend to answer as requested rather than discover on reviewing your paper that you *listed without describing*, that you selected the *worst* choice rather than the *best* choice, etc.

3) If the examination is of the objective or multiple-choice type – that is, each question will also give a series of possible answers: A, B, C or D, and you are called upon to select the best answer and write the letter next to that answer on your answer paper – it is advisable to start answering each question in turn. There may be anywhere from 50 to 100 such questions in the three or four hours allotted and you can see how much time would be taken if you read through all the questions before beginning to answer any. Furthermore, if you come across a question or group of questions which you know would be difficult to answer, it would undoubtedly affect your handling of all the other questions.

4) If the examination is of the essay type and contains but a few questions, it is a moot point as to whether you should read all the questions before starting to answer any one. Of course, if you are given a choice – say five out of seven and the like – then it is essential to read all the questions so you can eliminate the two that are most difficult. If, however, you are asked to answer all the questions, there may be danger in trying to answer the easiest one first because you may find that you will spend too much time on it. The best technique is to answer the first question, then proceed to the second, etc.

5) Time your answers. Before the exam begins, write down the time it started, then add the time allowed for the examination and write down the time it must be completed, then divide the time available somewhat as follows:
   - If 3-1/2 hours are allowed, that would be 210 minutes. If you have 80 objective-type questions, that would be an average of 2-1/2 minutes per question. Allow yourself no more than 2 minutes per question, or a total of 160 minutes, which will permit about 50 minutes to review.
   - If for the time allotment of 210 minutes there are 7 essay questions to answer, that would average about 30 minutes a question. Give yourself only 25 minutes per question so that you have about 35 minutes to review.

6) The most important instruction is to *read each question* and make sure you know what is wanted. The second most important instruction is to *time yourself properly* so that you answer every question. The third most important instruction is to *answer every question*. Guess if you have to but include something for each question. Remember that you will receive no credit for a blank and will probably receive some credit if you write something in answer to an essay question. If you guess a letter – say "B" for a multiple-choice question – you may have guessed right. If you leave a blank as an answer to a multiple-choice question, the examiners may respect your feelings but it will not add a point to your score. Some exams may penalize you for wrong answers, so in such cases *only*, you may not want to guess unless you have some basis for your answer.

7) Suggestions
   a. Objective-type questions
      1. Examine the question booklet for proper sequence of pages and questions
      2. Read all instructions carefully
      3. Skip any question which seems too difficult; return to it after all other questions have been answered
      4. Apportion your time properly; do not spend too much time on any single question or group of questions

5. Note and underline key words – *all, most, fewest, least, best, worst, same, opposite*, etc.
6. Pay particular attention to negatives
7. Note unusual option, e.g., unduly long, short, complex, different or similar in content to the body of the question
8. Observe the use of "hedging" words – *probably, may, most likely*, etc.
9. Make sure that your answer is put next to the same number as the question
10. Do not second-guess unless you have good reason to believe the second answer is definitely more correct
11. Cross out original answer if you decide another answer is more accurate; do not erase until you are ready to hand your paper in
12. Answer all questions; guess unless instructed otherwise
13. Leave time for review

b. Essay questions
   1. Read each question carefully
   2. Determine exactly what is wanted. Underline key words or phrases.
   3. Decide on outline or paragraph answer
   4. Include many different points and elements unless asked to develop any one or two points or elements
   5. Show impartiality by giving pros and cons unless directed to select one side only
   6. Make and write down any assumptions you find necessary to answer the questions
   7. Watch your English, grammar, punctuation and choice of words
   8. Time your answers; don't crowd material

8) Answering the essay question

Most essay questions can be answered by framing the specific response around several key words or ideas. Here are a few such key words or ideas:

M's: manpower, materials, methods, money, management
P's: purpose, program, policy, plan, procedure, practice, problems, pitfalls, personnel, public relations

   a. Six basic steps in handling problems:
      1. Preliminary plan and background development
      2. Collect information, data and facts
      3. Analyze and interpret information, data and facts
      4. Analyze and develop solutions as well as make recommendations
      5. Prepare report and sell recommendations
      6. Install recommendations and follow up effectiveness

   b. Pitfalls to avoid
      1. *Taking things for granted* – A statement of the situation does not necessarily imply that each of the elements is necessarily true; for example, a complaint may be invalid and biased so that all that can be taken for granted is that a complaint has been registered

2. *Considering only one side of a situation* – Wherever possible, indicate several alternatives and then point out the reasons you selected the best one
3. *Failing to indicate follow up* – Whenever your answer indicates action on your part, make certain that you will take proper follow-up action to see how successful your recommendations, procedures or actions turn out to be
4. *Taking too long in answering any single question* – Remember to time your answers properly

IX. AFTER THE TEST

Scoring procedures differ in detail among civil service jurisdictions although the general principles are the same. Whether the papers are hand-scored or graded by machine we have described, they are nearly always graded by number. That is, the person who marks the paper knows only the number – never the name – of the applicant. Not until all the papers have been graded will they be matched with names. If other tests, such as training and experience or oral interview ratings have been given, scores will be combined. Different parts of the examination usually have different weights. For example, the written test might count 60 percent of the final grade, and a rating of training and experience 40 percent. In many jurisdictions, veterans will have a certain number of points added to their grades.

After the final grade has been determined, the names are placed in grade order and an eligible list is established. There are various methods for resolving ties between those who get the same final grade – probably the most common is to place first the name of the person whose application was received first. Job offers are made from the eligible list in the order the names appear on it. You will be notified of your grade and your rank as soon as all these computations have been made. This will be done as rapidly as possible.

People who are found to meet the requirements in the announcement are called "eligibles." Their names are put on a list of eligible candidates. An eligible's chances of getting a job depend on how high he stands on this list and how fast agencies are filling jobs from the list.

When a job is to be filled from a list of eligibles, the agency asks for the names of people on the list of eligibles for that job. When the civil service commission receives this request, it sends to the agency the names of the three people highest on this list. Or, if the job to be filled has specialized requirements, the office sends the agency the names of the top three persons who meet these requirements from the general list.

The appointing officer makes a choice from among the three people whose names were sent to him. If the selected person accepts the appointment, the names of the others are put back on the list to be considered for future openings.

That is the rule in hiring from all kinds of eligible lists, whether they are for typist, carpenter, chemist, or something else. For every vacancy, the appointing officer has his choice of any one of the top three eligibles on the list. This explains why the person whose name is on top of the list sometimes does not get an appointment when some of the persons lower on the list do. If the appointing officer chooses the second or third eligible, the No. 1 eligible does not get a job at once, but stays on the list until he is appointed or the list is terminated.

X. HOW TO PASS THE INTERVIEW TEST

The examination for which you applied requires an oral interview test. You have already taken the written test and you are now being called for the interview test – the final part of the formal examination.

You may think that it is not possible to prepare for an interview test and that there are no procedures to follow during an interview. Our purpose is to point out some things you can do in advance that will help you and some good rules to follow and pitfalls to avoid while you are being interviewed.

What is an interview supposed to test?

The written examination is designed to test the technical knowledge and competence of the candidate; the oral is designed to evaluate intangible qualities, not readily measured otherwise, and to establish a list showing the relative fitness of each candidate – as measured against his competitors – for the position sought. Scoring is not on the basis of "right" and "wrong," but on a sliding scale of values ranging from "not passable" to "outstanding." As a matter of fact, it is possible to achieve a relatively low score without a single "incorrect" answer because of evident weakness in the qualities being measured.

Occasionally, an examination may consist entirely of an oral test – either an individual or a group oral. In such cases, information is sought concerning the technical knowledges and abilities of the candidate, since there has been no written examination for this purpose. More commonly, however, an oral test is used to supplement a written examination.

Who conducts interviews?

The composition of oral boards varies among different jurisdictions. In nearly all, a representative of the personnel department serves as chairman. One of the members of the board may be a representative of the department in which the candidate would work. In some cases, "outside experts" are used, and, frequently, a businessman or some other representative of the general public is asked to serve. Labor and management or other special groups may be represented. The aim is to secure the services of experts in the appropriate field.

However the board is composed, it is a good idea (and not at all improper or unethical) to ascertain in advance of the interview who the members are and what groups they represent. When you are introduced to them, you will have some idea of their backgrounds and interests, and at least you will not stutter and stammer over their names.

What should be done before the interview?

While knowledge about the board members is useful and takes some of the surprise element out of the interview, there is other preparation which is more substantive. It *is* possible to prepare for an oral interview – in several ways:

1) Keep a copy of your application and review it carefully before the interview

This may be the only document before the oral board, and the starting point of the interview. Know what education and experience you have listed there, and the sequence and dates of all of it. Sometimes the board will ask you to review the highlights of your experience for them; you should not have to hem and haw doing it.

2) Study the class specification and the examination announcement

Usually, the oral board has one or both of these to guide them. The qualities, characteristics or knowledges required by the position sought are stated in these documents. They offer valuable clues as to the nature of the oral interview. For example, if the job involves supervisory responsibilities, the announcement will usually indicate that knowledge of modern supervisory methods and the qualifications of the candidate as a supervisor will be tested. If so, you can expect such questions, frequently in the form of a hypothetical situation which you are expected to solve. NEVER go into an oral without knowledge of the duties and responsibilities of the job you seek.

3) Think through each qualification required

Try to visualize the kind of questions you would ask if you were a board member. How well could you answer them? Try especially to appraise your own knowledge and background in each area, *measured against the job sought*, and identify any areas in which you are weak. Be critical and realistic – do not flatter yourself.

4) Do some general reading in areas in which you feel you may be weak

For example, if the job involves supervision and your past experience has NOT, some general reading in supervisory methods and practices, particularly in the field of human relations, might be useful. Do NOT study agency procedures or detailed manuals. The oral board will be testing your understanding and capacity, not your memory.

5) Get a good night's sleep and watch your general health and mental attitude

You will want a clear head at the interview. Take care of a cold or any other minor ailment, and of course, no hangovers.

What should be done on the day of the interview?

Now comes the day of the interview itself. Give yourself plenty of time to get there. Plan to arrive somewhat ahead of the scheduled time, particularly if your appointment is in the fore part of the day. If a previous candidate fails to appear, the board might be ready for you a bit early. By early afternoon an oral board is almost invariably behind schedule if there are many candidates, and you may have to wait. Take along a book or magazine to read, or your application to review, but leave any extraneous material in the waiting room when you go in for your interview. In any event, relax and compose yourself.

The matter of dress is important. The board is forming impressions about you – from your experience, your manners, your attitude, and your appearance. Give your personal appearance careful attention. Dress your best, but not your flashiest. Choose conservative, appropriate clothing, and be sure it is immaculate. This is a business interview, and your appearance should indicate that you regard it as such. Besides, being well groomed and properly dressed will help boost your confidence.

Sooner or later, someone will call your name and escort you into the interview room. *This is it.* From here on you are on your own. It is too late for any more preparation. But remember, you asked for this opportunity to prove your fitness, and you are here because your request was granted.

What happens when you go in?

The usual sequence of events will be as follows: The clerk (who is often the board stenographer) will introduce you to the chairman of the oral board, who will introduce you to the other members of the board. Acknowledge the introductions before you sit down. Do not be surprised if you find a microphone facing you or a stenotypist sitting by. Oral interviews are usually recorded in the event of an appeal or other review.

Usually the chairman of the board will open the interview by reviewing the highlights of your education and work experience from your application – primarily for the benefit of the other members of the board, as well as to get the material into the record. Do not interrupt or comment unless there is an error or significant misinterpretation; if that is the case, do not hesitate. But do not quibble about insignificant matters. Also, he will usually ask you some question about your education, experience or your present job – partly to get you to start talking and to establish the interviewing "rapport." He may start the actual questioning, or turn it over to one of the other members. Frequently, each member undertakes the questioning on a particular area, one in which he is perhaps most competent, so you can expect each member to participate in the examination. Because time is limited, you may also expect some rather abrupt switches in the direction the questioning takes, so do not be upset by it. Normally, a board member will not pursue a single line of questioning unless he discovers a particular strength or weakness.

After each member has participated, the chairman will usually ask whether any member has any further questions, then will ask you if you have anything you wish to add. Unless you are expecting this question, it may floor you. Worse, it may start you off on an extended, extemporaneous speech. The board is not usually seeking more information. The question is principally to offer you a last opportunity to present further qualifications or to indicate that you have nothing to add. So, if you feel that a significant qualification or characteristic has been overlooked, it is proper to point it out in a sentence or so. Do not compliment the board on the thoroughness of their examination – they have been sketchy, and you know it. If you wish, merely say, "No thank you, I have nothing further to add." This is a point where you can "talk yourself out" of a good impression or fail to present an important bit of information. Remember, *you close the interview yourself*.

The chairman will then say, "That is all, Mr. _____, thank you." Do not be startled; the interview is over, and quicker than you think. Thank him, gather your belongings and take your leave. Save your sigh of relief for the other side of the door.

How to put your best foot forward

Throughout this entire process, you may feel that the board individually and collectively is trying to pierce your defenses, seek out your hidden weaknesses and embarrass and confuse you. Actually, this is not true. They are obliged to make an appraisal of your qualifications for the job you are seeking, and they want to see you in your best light. Remember, they must interview all candidates and a non-cooperative candidate may become a failure in spite of their best efforts to bring out his qualifications. Here are 15 suggestions that will help you:

1) Be natural – Keep your attitude confident, not cocky

If you are not confident that you can do the job, do not expect the board to be. Do not apologize for your weaknesses, try to bring out your strong points. The board is interested in a positive, not negative, presentation. Cockiness will antagonize any board member and make him wonder if you are covering up a weakness by a false show of strength.

2) Get comfortable, but don't lounge or sprawl

Sit erectly but not stiffly. A careless posture may lead the board to conclude that you are careless in other things, or at least that you are not impressed by the importance of the occasion. Either conclusion is natural, even if incorrect. Do not fuss with your clothing, a pencil or an ashtray. Your hands may occasionally be useful to emphasize a point; do not let them become a point of distraction.

3) Do not wisecrack or make small talk

This is a serious situation, and your attitude should show that you consider it as such. Further, the time of the board is limited – they do not want to waste it, and neither should you.

4) Do not exaggerate your experience or abilities

In the first place, from information in the application or other interviews and sources, the board may know more about you than you think. Secondly, you probably will not get away with it. An experienced board is rather adept at spotting such a situation, so do not take the chance.

5) If you know a board member, do not make a point of it, yet do not hide it

Certainly you are not fooling him, and probably not the other members of the board. Do not try to take advantage of your acquaintanceship – it will probably do you little good.

6) Do not dominate the interview

Let the board do that. They will give you the clues – do not assume that you have to do all the talking. Realize that the board has a number of questions to ask you, and do not try to take up all the interview time by showing off your extensive knowledge of the answer to the first one.

7) Be attentive

You only have 20 minutes or so, and you should keep your attention at its sharpest throughout. When a member is addressing a problem or question to you, give him your undivided attention. Address your reply principally to him, but do not exclude the other board members.

8) Do not interrupt

A board member may be stating a problem for you to analyze. He will ask you a question when the time comes. Let him state the problem, and wait for the question.

9) Make sure you understand the question

Do not try to answer until you are sure what the question is. If it is not clear, restate it in your own words or ask the board member to clarify it for you. However, do not haggle about minor elements.

10) Reply promptly but not hastily

A common entry on oral board rating sheets is "candidate responded readily," or "candidate hesitated in replies." Respond as promptly and quickly as you can, but do not jump to a hasty, ill-considered answer.

11) Do not be peremptory in your answers

A brief answer is proper – but do not fire your answer back. That is a losing game from your point of view. The board member can probably ask questions much faster than you can answer them.

12) Do not try to create the answer you think the board member wants

He is interested in what kind of mind you have and how it works – not in playing games. Furthermore, he can usually spot this practice and will actually grade you down on it.

13) Do not switch sides in your reply merely to agree with a board member

Frequently, a member will take a contrary position merely to draw you out and to see if you are willing and able to defend your point of view. Do not start a debate, yet do not surrender a good position. If a position is worth taking, it is worth defending.

14) Do not be afraid to admit an error in judgment if you are shown to be wrong

The board knows that you are forced to reply without any opportunity for careful consideration. Your answer may be demonstrably wrong. If so, admit it and get on with the interview.

15) Do not dwell at length on your present job

The opening question may relate to your present assignment. Answer the question but do not go into an extended discussion. You are being examined for a *new* job, not your present one. As a matter of fact, try to phrase ALL your answers in terms of the job for which you are being examined.

Basis of Rating

Probably you will forget most of these "do's" and "don'ts" when you walk into the oral interview room. Even remembering them all will not ensure you a passing grade. Perhaps you did not have the qualifications in the first place. But remembering them will help you to put your best foot forward, without treading on the toes of the board members.

Rumor and popular opinion to the contrary notwithstanding, an oral board wants you to make the best appearance possible. They know you are under pressure – but they also want to see how you respond to it as a guide to what your reaction would be under the pressures of the job you seek. They will be influenced by the degree of poise you display, the personal traits you show and the manner in which you respond.

ABOUT THIS BOOK

This book contains tests divided into Examination Sections. Go through each test, answering every question in the margin. We have also attached a sample answer sheet at the back of the book that can be removed and used. At the end of each test look at the answer key and check your answers. On the ones you got wrong, look at the right answer choice and learn. Do not fill in the answers first. Do not memorize the questions and answers, but understand the answer and principles involved. On your test, the questions will likely be different from the samples. Questions are changed and new ones added. If you understand these past questions you should have success with any changes that arise. Tests may consist of several types of questions. We have additional books on each subject should more study be advisable or necessary for you. Finally, the more you study, the better prepared you will be. This book is intended to be the last thing you study before you walk into the examination room. Prior study of relevant texts is also recommended. NLC publishes some of these in our Fundamental Series. Knowledge and good sense are important factors in passing your exam. Good luck also helps. So now study this Passbook, absorb the material contained within and take that knowledge into the examination. Then do your best to pass that exam.

EXAMINATION SECTION

EXAMINATION SECTION
TEST 1

DIRECTIONS: Each question or incomplete statement is followed by several suggested answers or completions. Select the one that BEST answers the question or completes the statement. *PRINT THE LETTER OF THE CORRECT ANSWER IN THE SPACE AT THE RIGHT.*

1. The liquid portion of an anticoagulated blood specimen is termed   1.____

   A. serum   B. exudate   C. plasma   D. fibrin

2. Which of the following is NOT an element of whole blood?   2.____

   A. Cells   B. Tissue   C. Water   D. Solutes

3. During the analysis of vacuum tubes containing whole blood, the most effective procedure for preventing undesired clotting is   3.____

   A. using a smaller amount of additive
   B. mixing the tubes well by inversion
   C. venting the tube while inserting the stopper
   D. centrifuging at a higher speed

4. The term *acrocyanosis* refers to   4.____

   A. a tumor of glandular superficial epithelium
   B. a ballooning-out of the wall of a vein, an artery, or the heart due to weakening of the wall by disease, injury, or congenital defect
   C. formation of a blood clot in the blood vessels that supply the extremities
   D. a blueness of the hands or feet caused by disturbances of the superficial veins

5. What is the term for a solid mass derived from blood constituents that can occlude a blood vessel?   5.____

   A. Hemolyzed RBC   B. Embolus
   C. Triglyceride   D. Thrombus

6. Of the following, which method for requesting a laboratory test is most likely to be error-free?   6.____

   A. Computerized   B. Verbal
   C. Handwritten requisition   D. Verbal stat

7. Among professionals, it is generally agreed that the most important step in the performance of a venipuncture is the   7.____

   A. proper positioning of a patient
   B. selection of a properly sized needle
   C. selection of a venipuncture site
   D. positive identification of the patient by name

8. A calcium test can be useful in each of the following ways EXCEPT for detecting   8.____

   A. endocrine disorders   B. acid-base imbalance
   C. hepatic disease   D. blood-clotting deficiencies

9. The life span of a red blood cell is typically between _____ days.　　　　9.____

   A. 5 and 10　　　　　　　　　　　B. 30 and 90
   C. 100 and 120　　　　　　　　　　D. 180 and 200

10. During any blood collection procedure, a tourniquet should be placed around the　10.____
    patient's arm

    A. as close to the collection site as possible
    B. for no more than one minute
    C. until the needle is removed
    D. until the entire procedure is completed

11. Inflammation of a vein, often accompanied by clot formation, is known as　　11.____

    A. aneurysm　　　　　　　　　　　B. phlebitis
    C. thrombosis　　　　　　　　　　　D. sclerosis

12. Of the following, which may be used to diagnose whooping cough in infants and children?　12.____

    A. CSF culture　　　　　　　　　　B. Stool sample
    C. Nasopharyngeal culture　　　　　D. Urine sample

13. Among the following, which laboratory-acquired infection most commonly occurs?　13.____

    A. Streptococcus　　　　　　　　　B. HBV
    C. Tuberculosis　　　　　　　　　　D. HIV

14. Gloves worn in the workplace to prevent infection are typically made from each of the following materials EXCEPT　14.____

    A. nitryl　　　B. leather　　　C. rubber　　　D. latex

15. The _____ system is the body's primary regulator of hormones.　　　　15.____

    A. lymphatic　　　　　　　　　　　B. reproductive
    C. nervous　　　　　　　　　　　　D. endocrine

16. The purpose of an Allen test is to determine　　　　　　　　　　　　　16.____

    A. collateral circulation between radial and ulnar arteries
    B. blood pressure
    C. oxygen concentration
    D. the likelihood of hematoma

17. During venipuncture, the _____ may result in a hematoma.　　　　　　17.____

    A. insertion of the needle through the vein
    B. occlusion of a needle
    C. positioning of the needle bevel against the vein wall
    D. partial insertion of the needle bevel in the vein

18. Which of the following veins is NOT commonly used for venipuncture procedures?   18.____

    A. Brachial   B. Cephalic
    C. Basilic   D. Median cubital

19. The needle gauge most often used during venipuncture procedures is   19.____

    A. 16   B. 18   C. 21   D. 23

Question 20-25.

DIRECTIONS: Questions 20 through 25 refer to the figure below, a cross-section of an artery. Place the letter that corresponds to each diagrammed element in the space at the right.

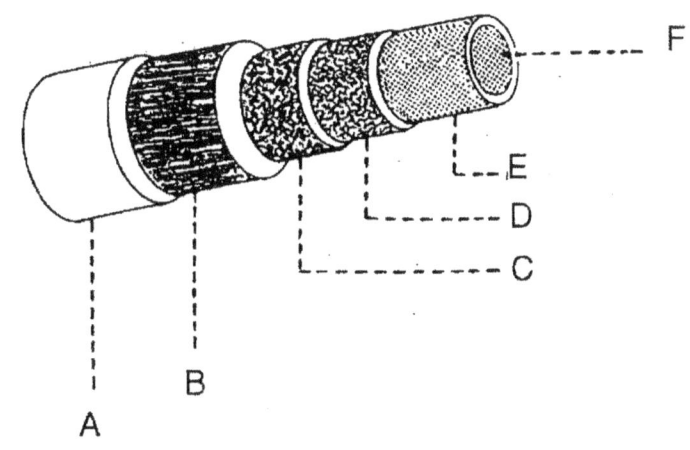

20. Tunica media   20.____

21. Lumen   21.____

22. Elastin   22.____

23. Connective tissue   23.____

24. Tunica externa   24.____

25. Endothelial cells   25.____

KEY (CORRECT ANSWERS)

1.	C	11.	B
2.	B	12.	C
3.	B	13.	B
4.	D	14.	B
5.	D	15.	D
6.	A	16.	A
7.	D	17.	D
8.	C	18.	A
9.	C	19.	C
10.	B	20.	B

21. F
22. C
23. D
24. A
25. E

TEST 2

DIRECTIONS: Each question or incomplete statement is followed by several suggested answers or completions. Select the one that BEST answers the question or completes the statement. *PRINT THE LETTER OF THE CORRECT ANSWER IN THE SPACE AT THE RIGHT.*

1. Which of the following procedures is involved in a finger puncture? 1.____

    A. Collecting the first drop
    B. Puncturing at an angle to the fingerprint
    C. Using a butterfly needle
    D. Puncturing parallel to the fingerprint

2. Which of the following types of blood cells typically stain bluish with neutral dyes? 2.____

    A. Basophils   B. Eosinophils
    C. Monocytes   D. Neutrophils

3. An amylase test is used to detect 3.____

    A. pancreatitis   B. prostatic cancer
    C. severe hepatic disease D. acid-base balance

4. Which of the following infections is NOT typically spread by means of vector-borne transmission? 4.____

    A. Encephalitis   B. Malaria
    C. coli   D. Lyme disease

5. Which of the following lancet lengths (mm) should be used for capillary collection from newborns? 5.____

    A. 2.40   B. 2.75   C. 3.25   D. 3.75

6. Which of the following is a granulocyte? 6.____

    A. Monocyte   B. Basophil
    C. Lymphocyte   D. Erythrocyte

7. The first stage in the coagulation process is the _____ phase. 7.____

    A. clot-retraction   B. platelet
    C. vascular   D. coagulation

8. Which of the following methods would be preferred for collecting blood from a newborn patient? 8.____

    A. Finger stick   B. Dorsal hand venipuncture
    C. Antecubital fossa venipuncture D. Ankle stick

9. Which of the following abbreviations, commonly used in medical recordkeeping, means *before meals*? 9.____

    A. ac   B. pe   C. bm   D. pc

5

10. A patient under airborne precautions should have _____ air exchanges per hour.   10.____

    A. 1-2   B. 3-4   C. 6-12   D. 10-15

11. A specimen collected for the purpose of determining _____ should be protected from light.   11.____

    A. glucose level   B. blood urea nitrogen (BUN)
    C. bilirubin content   D. hemoglobin level

12. Which of the following produces red blood cells?   12.____
    I. Spleen
    II. Bone marrow
    III. Thymus
    IV. Lymph nodes
    The CORRECT answer is:

    A. I only   B. II only   C. II, III   D. III, IV

13. Which of the following laboratory tests is used to detect gout and kidney dysfunction?   13.____

    A. Lipase   B. Blood urea nitrogen (BUN)
    C. Ferritin   D. Uric acid

14. If each of the following draws is to be performed during a single venipuncture, and an evacuated system is used, which should be performed FIRST?   14.____

    A. Plain red-topped tubes   B. Citrate-containing tubes
    C. Blood culture   D. Heparin-containing tubes

15. Other than the index finger, which of the following is used most often for skin puncture?   15.____

    A. Thumb   B. Third (middle) finger
    C. Fourth (ring) finger   D. Fifth (pinky) finger

16. Which of the following is a germ cell?   16.____

    A. Red blood cell   B. T-cell
    C. Sperm   D. Neurons

17. Which of the following anticoagulants works by precipitating calcium from the blood?   17.____

    A. SPS   B. Sodium oxalate
    C. Lithium heparin D. EDTA

18. The most numerous type of cell in circulating blood is the   18.____

    A. thrombocyte   B. macrophage
    C. erythrocyte   D. leukocyte

19. Which of the following specimens is NOT typically used in forensic analysis?   19.____

    A. Nails   B. Stool   C. Urine   D. Hair

20. Which of the following is not a source of preanalytic error in medical recordkeeping?   20.____

    A. Patient variables   B. Physician's attitude
    C. Processing variables   D. Specimen variables

21. Which of the following organs produces insulin?

    A. Liver
    B. Gallbladder
    C. Pancreas
    D. Spleen

22. If red blood cells are described as *crenated,* it means they are

    A. bluish in tint
    B. elongated
    C. notched
    D. sickle-shaped

23. If a technician receives a short draw from an attempt at blood collection with an evacuated system, which of the following is NOT likely to be a remedy?

    A. Checking the tube vacuum
    B. Balancing the centrifuge
    C. Using a tube that has not expired
    D. Redrawing the specimen, being careful not to miss the vein

24. Which of the following analyte results is most likely to be affected by a patient's taking high doses of acetaminophen?

    A. Blood urea nitrogen (BUN)
    B. Serum bilirubin
    C. Blood glucose
    D. CPK

25. Which of the following abbreviations, commonly used in medical recordkeeping, means *as required*?

    A. hs
    B. PP
    C. per
    D. prn

KEY (CORRECT ANSWERS)

1. B		11. C	
2. D		12. B	
3. A		13. D	
4. C		14. C	
5. A		15. B	
6. B		16. C	
7. C		17. B	
8. B		18. C	
9. A		19. B	
10. C		20. B	

21. C
22. C
23. B
24. B
25. D

EXAMINATION SECTION
TEST 1

DIRECTIONS: Each question or incomplete statement is followed by several suggested answers or completions. Select the one that BEST answers the question or completes the statement. *PRINT THE LETTER OF THE CORRECT ANSWER IN THE SPACE AT THE RIGHT.*

Questions 1-10.

DIRECTIONS: Questions 1 through 10 require you to match purposes or characteristics with the appropriate color of a stopper used with tubes in an evacuated blood collection system. Choosing from the list at the right, place the letter that corresponds with the purpose or characteristic in the appropriate space at the right.

1. Red
2. Yellow
3. Light blue
4. Green
5. Brown
6. Red-gray
7. Lavender
8. Green-gray
9. Gray
10. Royal blue

A. Uses an acid-citrate-dextrose additive
B. Used for the collection of whole blood for hematology determination
C. Recommended for blood banking and therapeutic drug levels
D. Contains a glycolytic inhibitor
E. For the collection of plasma for blood lead determinations
F. For the collection of plasma or serum for determinations such as nutrient studies
G. For the collection of whole blood for coagulation determinations
H. Uses both lithium heparin and polymer gel as additives; used for separating plasma from cells
I. For the collection of plasma for chemistry determinations
J. For the collection of serum; used for separating serum from cells

1.____
2.____
3.____
4.____
5.____
6.____
7.____
8.____
9.____
10.____

11. When using two glass slides to make a blood smear, the best angle is approximately _____ degrees. 11.____

    A. 15   B. 30   C. 45   D. 90

12. Structural components of quality in specimen collection include each of the following EXCEPT

    A. sufficiency of supplies
    B. expiration dates
    C. number of sticks
    D. condition of supplies

13. Which of the following laboratory tests is used to evaluate red blood cell production?

    A. Reticulocyte count
    B. Hematocrit
    C. Red blood count (RBC)
    D. Iron

14. When a syringe is used to draw arterial blood, what volume of heparin should be used for each milliliter of blood drawn?

    A. 0.01   B. 0.05   C. 0.10   D. 0.25

15. For which of the following patients would protective isolation most likely be used? A(n)

    A. pediatric patient with an immunodeficiency
    B. pediatric patient with whooping cough
    C. adult with active tuberculosis
    D. adult with meningitis

16. After the skin is punctured to obtain blood for glucose monitoring, the technician should

    A. gently squeeze the patient's finger to enlarge the first drop for the test
    B. use a sterile gauze to remove the first drop of blood
    C. collect the first drop of blood for the glucose test
    D. use an alcohol pad to remove the first drop of blood

17. Which of the following abbreviations is commonly used in clinical laboratories to denote a *full complement*?

    A. Hct   B. C50/C100   C. Rh   D. C3/C4

18. Which of the following is NOT an ion commonly found in the blood?

    A. Calcium   B. Magnesium   C. Lithium   D. Chloride

19. Serum should be separated from blood cells as soon as blood is collected from a patient in order to

    A. prevent glycolysis
    B. avoid homeostasis
    C. prevent hemoconcentration
    D. avoid hemolysis

20. The purpose of a chain-of-custody process is to

    A. identify specimens
    B. ensure donor privacy
    C. maintain control and accountability of a specimen from collection to final results
    D. ensure that the specimen matches the donor

21. During a bleeding time test, it is customary to maintain the sphygmomanomater at a pressure of _____ mmHg throughout the test.

   A. 20   B. 40   C. 60   D. 80

22. Which of the following is NOT a function of an osmolality test?

   A. Evaluating hydration
   B. Measuring the severity of anemia
   C. Detecting liver disease
   D. Evaluating electrolyte levels

23. Which of the following is typically largest in size?

   A. Heme
   B. Platelet
   C. Red blood cell
   D. White blood cell

24. A patient must fast for _____ hours prior to a timed blood glucose level determination.

   A. 6 to 8
   B. 8 to 12
   C. 12 to 16
   D. 16 to 24

25. For which of the following patients would contact isolation be most appropriate?

   A. Patients with diarrheal diseases
   B. Patients with postoperative catheters
   C. Patients with whooping cough
   D. Pediatric patients with acute respiratory infections

KEY (CORRECT ANSWERS)

1.	C	11.	B
2.	A	12.	C
3.	G	13.	A
4.	I	14.	B
5.	E	15.	A
6.	J	16.	B
7.	B	17.	B
8.	H	18.	C
9.	D	19.	D
10.	F	20.	C

21. B
22. B
23. D
24. B
25. D

TEST 2

DIRECTIONS: Each question or incomplete statement is followed by several suggested answers or completions. Select the one that BEST answers the question or completes the statement. *PRINT THE LETTER OF THE CORRECT ANSWER IN THE SPACE AT THE RIGHT.*

1. A patient described as *febrile*

    A. is prone to seizure
    B. has a fever
    C. has an abnormal tube-like canal extending from one organ to another
    D. is experiencing abnormal heart muscle contractions

    1._____

2. Anemia is generally defined as a level of hemoglobin in the blood that is _____ grams/dL or less

    A. 1   B. 7   C. 12   D. 18

    2._____

3. Of the types of cells listed below, which have no nucleus?

    A. Eosinophils   B. Basophils
    C. Erythrocytes   D. Neutrophils

    3._____

4. The standard and transmission-based precautions currently used in today's health care workplace were recommended in 1995 by

    A. HCFA   B. CDC   C. HICPAC   D. OSHA

    4._____

5. What type of body fluid is extracted from joint cavities?

    A. Bursal   B. Synovial
    C. Interstitial   D. Peritoneal

    5._____

6. Which of the following laboratory tests is useful in the detection of skeletal disease?

    A. Folic acid   B. Bilirubin
    C. Alkaline phosphatase   D. Creatinine

    6._____

7. Laboratory analysis of a blood specimen, collected into an evacuated system with an EDTA additive, reveals a false low white cell count and platelet count. The most likely cause of this is

    A. positive pressure within the vacuum tube
    B. excess additive in the specimen due to a short draw
    C. clotting due to insufficient mixing of specimen with additive
    D. hemolysis

    7._____

8. During an arterial puncture that is performed for ABG determination, the needle should be inserted at an angle of at least _____ degrees.

    A. 15   B. 30   C. 45   D. 60

    8._____

9. Laboratory tests of a blood specimen reveal fibrin strands in tubes that are intended to hold serum. The most likely cause is

   A. insufficient tube vacuum
   B. insufficient clotting time before centrifugation
   C. unbalanced centrifuge
   D. hemolysis

9._____

10. A green-topped blood collection vacuum tube uses an additive of

    A. lithium heparin
    B. ammonium oxalate
    C. sodium heparin
    D. EDTA

10._____

11. Each of the following tests can be measured by electrolyte monitoring through point-of-care testing EXCEPT

    A. pCO_2
    B. Na^+
    C. HCO_3^-
    D. Cl^-

11._____

12. Which of the following is a specific term used to denote the study of blood serum for antigen-antibody reactions?

    A. Hepatology
    B. Serology
    C. Thrombology
    D. Nephrology

12._____

13. The ideal position of the arm during a venipuncture procedure is

    A. slightly bent, with the hand prone
    B. slightly bent, with the hand supine
    C. in a straight line from shoulder to wrist
    D. bent 90°, with the hand supine

13._____

14. Which of the following is not a likely cause of hemoconcentration?

    A. Sclerotic veins
    B. Insertion of the needle at too shallow an angle
    C. Long-term IV therapy
    D. Excessive probing with the needle

14._____

15. The purpose of a bleeding-time test is to

    A. diagnose diabetes mellitus
    B. check for vascular abnormalities
    C. determine stores of liver glycogen
    D. diagnose hyperthyroidism

15._____

16. Which of the following vacuum tube sizes (diameter x length) has a draw volume of 7.0 ml?

    A. 10.25 mm x 64 mm
    B. 13 mm x 75 mm
    C. 13 mm x 100 mm
    D. 16 mm x 100 mm

16._____

17. Which of the following procedures would NOT typically be considered primary care?

    A. Prenatal examinations
    B. CAT scan
    C. Vaccinations
    D. Blood glucose screening

17._____

18. The MAIN difference between plasma and serum is that
    A. serum is a fluid
    B. serum contains leukocytes
    C. plasma contains fibrinogen
    D. plasma is clear in appearance

19. The abbreviation *qod,* appearing in a medical order, means
    A. daily
    B. every other day
    C. four times a day
    D. quantity not sufficient

20. On which of the following specimens is an O&P analysis performed?
    A. Urine
    B. CSF
    C. Amniotic fluid
    D. Stool

21. A _____-topped evacuated tube is preferred for the collection of a blood culture specimen.
    A. red-gray
    B. light blue
    C. gray
    D. yellow

22. The appearance of petachiae on a patient's arm are a signal to the phlebotomist that the
    A. needle has been inserted too far
    B. puncture site may bleed excessively
    C. patient is prone to seizure
    D. patient's vein has collapsed

23. A technician would NOT use the protein test in laboratory analysis for detecting
    A. hepatic function
    B. renal disorders
    C. hyperlipidemia
    D. protein deficiency

24. Which of the following is an immunohematology procedure?
    A. BUN
    B. Coombs' test
    C. AFB smear
    D. Sickle-cell preparation

25. If a patient is harmed while in the care of a phlebotomist, and it is determined that the harm could have been avoided, the phlebotomist is technically guilty of
    A. misfeasance
    B. negligence
    C. malpractice
    D. breach of duty

KEY (CORRECT ANSWERS)

1. B
2. B
3. C
4. C
5. B

6. C
7. C
8. C
9. B
10. C

11. A
12. B
13. C
14. B
15. B

16. C
17. B
18. C
19. B
20. D

21. D
22. B
23. C
24. B
25. D

EXAMINATION SECTION
TEST 1

DIRECTIONS: Each question or incomplete statement is followed by several suggested answers or completions. Select the one that BEST answers the question or completes the statement. *PRINT THE LETTER OF THE CORRECT ANSWER IN THE SPACE AT THE RIGHT.*

Questions 1-6.

DIRECTIONS: Questions 1 through 6 refer to the figure below, a diagram of the veins in the right arm (anterior view). Place the letter that corresponds to each diagrammed vein in the appropriate space at the right.

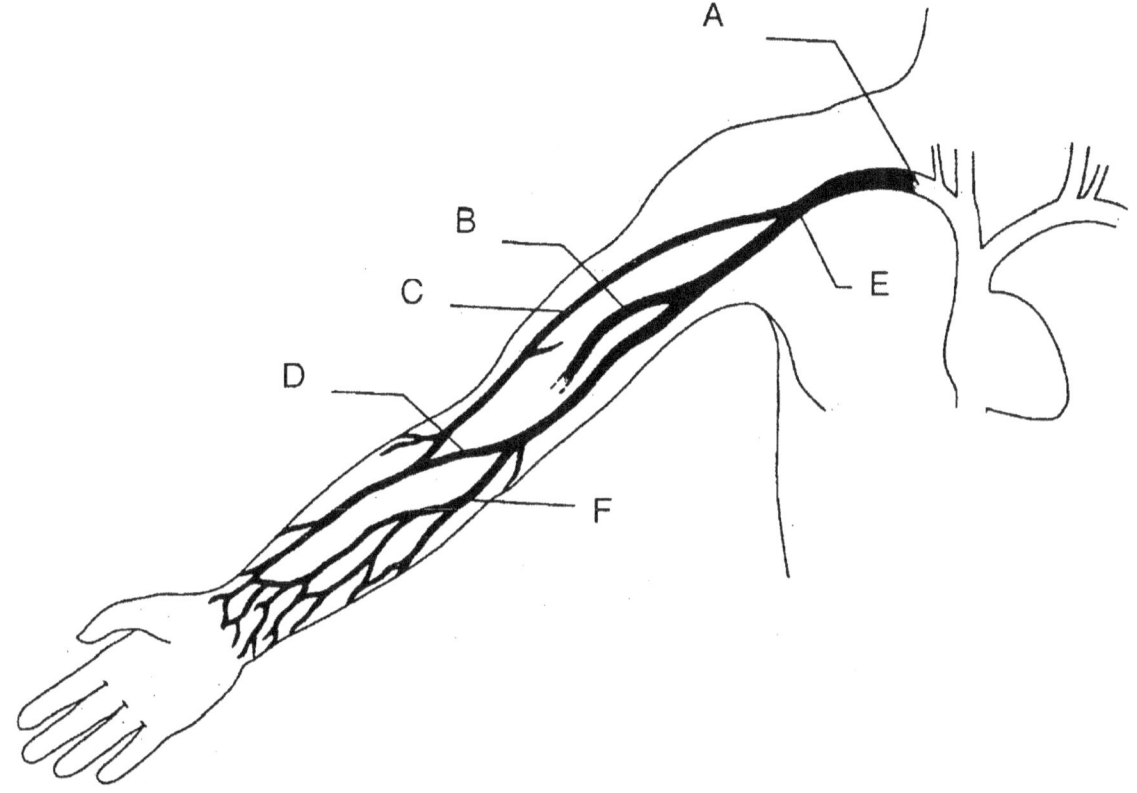

1. Axillary   1.____
2. Brachial   2.____
3. Cephalic   3.____
4. Median cubital   4.____
5. Subclavian   5.____
6. Basilic   6.____

7. In anatomic descriptions of the body, which of the following areas is divided into the thoracic, abdominal, and pelvic cavities?

   A. Sagittal
   B. Dorsal
   C. Transverse
   D. Ventral

8. Which of the following specimen types may require the use of both a polymer barrier and lithium heparin as additives?

   A. Whole blood
   B. Clotted blood/serum
   C. Urine
   D. Whole blood/plasma

9. A patient's heel might be warmed prior to a heel stick in order to

   A. accelerate hemostasis
   B. prevent hemoconcentration
   C. arterialize the blood
   D. prevent hemolysis

10. If each of the following draws is to be performed on a single patient using a syringe system, which would be performed last?

    A. EDTA-containing tubes
    B. Plain red-topped tubes
    C. Blood cultures
    D. Fluoride-containing tubes

11. Acidosis occurs when

    A. there is a shortage of CO_2 in the blood
    B. blood pH decreases to less than 7.35
    C. a patient suffers from excessive vomiting
    D. blood pH increases to more than 7.45

12. A GGT test is useful for each of the following EXCEPT

    A. detecting carcinoma of pancreas and liver
    B. diagnosing obstructive jaundice
    C. diagnosing hemolytic anemia
    D. diagnosing chronic alcoholic liver disease

13. Which of the following agencies has developed competency statements for phlebotomists?

    A. National Phlebotomy Association (NPA)
    B. American Society of Clinical Pathologists (ASCP) Board of Registry
    C. American Medical Technologists (AMT)
    D. American Society of Phlebotomy Technicians (ASPT)

14. Of the following items of equipment, which is used for skin punctures?

    A. AVL microsampler
    B. Tenderlett
    C. Autolet lite
    D. Samplette

15. Which of the following infections would require a phlebotomist to take off work entirely?

    A. Human immunodeficiency virus
    B. Herpes zoster

C. Hepatitis C
D. Conjunctivitis

16. The application of a tourniquet for an extended period of time is likely to produce a falsely elevated result in a test for

    A. glucose
    B. parathyroid hormone
    C. potassium
    D. bilirubin

17. Which of the following tests requires a minimum draw of 2 ml of blood?

    A. Histamine
    B. C-reactive protein
    C. Insulin
    D. Aldosterone

18. Which of the following body systems is NOT important for protection, support, or movement?

    A. Lymphatic
    B. Integumentary
    C. Muscular
    D. Skeletal

19. When using the Autolet platform for microcollection, it is important to remember that the shallowest incisions are made by devices that are color-coded

    A. orange   B. yellow   C. red   D. white

20. When a patient is under droplet precautions, a health care worker must wear a mask any time he or she is within _____ feet of the patient, or upon entering the room.

    A. 3   B. 10   C. 15   D. 20

21. Which branch of law is concerned with the use of education and planning for avoiding legal conflicts in blood collection?

    A. Civil
    B. Preparatory
    C. Administrative
    D. Preventive

22. From some manufacturers, a black-topped evacuated tube with buffered sodium citrate is available for blood collections used to determine

    A. CBC
    B. prostatic acid phosphatase (PAP)
    C. erythrocyte sedimentation rate (ESR)
    D. electrolyte levels

23. Which of the following is a laboratory test in which the red blood cells are centrifuged at a high speed so they will be separated from blood serum and their volume can be expressed as a percentage of total volume?

    A. Hematocrit
    B. White blood cell count (WBC)
    C. Blood urea nitrogen (BUN)
    D. Platelet count

24. A newborn patient weighs between 8-10 pounds. What is the maximum amount of blood (ml) that may be drawn from the patient at any one time?

    A. 2.5   B. 5   C. 10   D. 20

25. For which of the following tests would a skin puncture be used? 25.____

   A. Coagulation studies
   B. ESR determinations
   C. Routine hematology tests
   D. Blood cultures

KEY (CORRECT ANSWERS)

1.	E	11.	B
2.	B	12.	C
3.	C	13.	B
4.	D	14.	C
5.	A	15.	D
6.	F	16.	C
7.	D	17.	A
8.	D	18.	A
9.	C	19.	D
10.	B	20.	A

21. D
22. C
23. A
24. A
25. C

TEST 2

DIRECTIONS: Each question or incomplete statement is followed by several suggested answers or completions. Select the one that BEST answers the question or completes the statement. *PRINT THE LETTER OF THE CORRECT ANSWER IN THE SPACE AT THE RIGHT.*

1. A patient's hands are typically avoided as venipuncture sites for each of the following reasons EXCEPT
    A. a greater tendency for veins to roll
    B. slower healing of venipuncture site
    C. the abundant nerve supply
    D. the increased probability of infection

    1.____

2. Which of the following needle characteristics is denoted through the color coding system?
    A. Flexibility
    B. Gauge
    C. Length
    D. Additive

    2.____

3. What is the term for a series of chemical reactions in cells to change complex substances into simpler ones while simultaneously releasing energy?
    A. Homeostasis
    B. Catabolism
    C. Metabolism
    D. Anabolism

    3.____

4. Cold agglutinins in the blood tend to react most strongly at a temperature of
    A. 0   B. 4   C. 10   D. 22

    4.____

5. Which of the following types of blood cells typically stain dark purple or black with basic dyes?
    A. Basophils
    B. Eosinophils
    C. Monocytes
    D. Neutrophils

    5.____

6. During a venipuncture, the best angle for needle insertion is typically _____ degrees.
    A. 15   B. 30   C. 45   D. 60

    6.____

7. Which of the following is a significant purpose of Wright's stain?
    A. Identification of occult blood in stool specimens
    B. White blood cell differentiation
    C. Platelet counts
    D. Clarification of lipemic specimens

    7.____

8. Which of the following can be prevented by controlling the depth of lancet insertion during skin puncture?
    A. Osteomyelitis
    B. Puncturing a vein
    C. Hemoconcentration
    D. Excessive bleeding

    8.____

9. Which of the following represents the earliest stage in the development of a red blood cell?

    A. Reticulocyte
    B. Rubriblast
    C. Metarubricyte
    D. Prorubricyte

10. Which of the following tests would be ordered if a diagnosis of disseminated intravascular coagulation (DIC) needs to be determined?

    A. Prothrombin time (PT)
    B. Fibrin degradation products (FDP)
    C. Phosphorus
    D. Glucose tolerance (GTT)

11. Which of the following is a disinfectant?

    A. Chloramine
    B. Betadine
    C. Hydrogen peroxide
    D. Tincture of iodine

12. For which of the following reasons is blood from skin puncture more like arterial blood than venous blood?

    A. Venous pressure is greater in capillaries.
    B. The skin has a greater osmotic exposure to oxygen.
    C. The skin has more arterioles.
    D. More arterial blood flows in capillaries.

13. Which of the following statements is correctly worded in anatomic language?

    A. The eyes are inferior to the
    B. The toes are distal to the
    C. Muscle is superficial to skin.
    D. The arms are medial to the shoulders.

14. Which of the following diseases is identified through newborn blood screening?

    A. Hypothyroidism
    B. Syphilis
    C. Tuberculosis
    D. Cystic fibrosis

15. Which of the following is NOT a type of formal transmission-based precaution used in health care settings?

    A. Contact   B. Droplet   C. Vector   D. Airborne

16. If a blood specimen drawn into an evacuated system with a citrate additive presents a prolonged coagulation time, the most likely cause is

    A. the use of angle-head centrifuge
    B. an unbalanced centrifuge
    C. positive pressure in the tube
    D. a short draw

17. When a blood clot forms in a patient's circulatory system, the term used is

    A. phlebitis
    B. thrombosis
    C. coagulation
    D. embolus

18. Which of the following anticoagulants works by binding calcium?

   A. Sodium heparin
   B. Potassium oxalate
   C. Ammonium oxalate
   D. Sodium citrate

19. Which of the following is not a likely complication to the heel stick procedure?

   A. Abscess
   B. Calcification of nodules
   C. Osteomyelitis
   D. Foot paralysis

20. As a rule of thumb, blood samples should be transported to a clinical laboratory within _____ from the time of collection, in order to enable separation of serum or plasma from cells.

   A. 45 minutes
   B. 2 hours
   C. 12 hours
   D. 24 hours

21. Which of the following laboratory tests serves to confirm a diagnosis of diabetes mellitus or hypoglycemia?

   A. y-glutamyltransferase (GGT)
   B. Glucose (FBS)
   C. Triglycerides
   D. Glucose tolerance (GTT)

22. A unit of blood collected from a donor typically has a volume of about _____ ml.

   A. 150   B. 300   C. 450   D. 750

23. Which of the following infections is most likely to be spread through airborne transmission?

   A. Mycobacterium tuberculosis
   B. Human immunodeficiency virus (HIV)
   C. Salmonella
   D. Encephalitis

24. Arterial blood is the specimen of choice for each of the following tests EXCEPT

   A. pH
   B. prothrombin time
   C. CO_2 content
   D. O_2 content

25. A specimen collected for the purpose of determining _____ should be chilled.

   A. white blood count (WBC)
   B. blood gas
   C. glucose level
   D. bilirubin

KEY (CORRECT ANSWERS)

1.	B	11.	A
2.	C	12.	D
3.	B	13.	B
4.	B	14.	A
5.	A	15.	C
6.	A	16.	D
7.	B	17.	B
8.	A	18.	D
9.	B	19.	D
10.	B	20.	A

21. D
22. C
23. A
24. B
25. B

EXAMINATION SECTION
TEST 1

DIRECTIONS: Each question or incomplete statement is followed by several suggested answers or completions. Select the one that BEST answers the question or completes the statement. *PRINT THE LETTER OF THE CORRECT ANSWER IN THE SPACE AT THE RIGHT.*

1. Approximately what percentage of an adult's blood supply is composed of the liquid or fluid portion?

    A. 30   B. 45   C. 55   D. 70

2. When performing a finger stick, which of the following procedures is typically performed FIRST?

    A. Massaging the finger several times from base to tip
    B. Removing the lancet from the protective paper
    C. Cleaning the ball of the finger with an alcohol swab
    D. Wiping away the first drop of blood

3. Which of the following laboratory tests is useful for providing a differential diagnosis of myocardial or pulmonary infarction?

    A. Ammonia
    B. Cardiac isoenzymes
    C. Lactic dehydrogenase (LD/LDH)
    D. Coombs

4. Federal regulations require that employees who may have occupational exposure to blood contaminated with hepatitis B be offered a vaccine, at no cost, within _____ _____ after the employee has accepted the assignment.

    A. 24 hours   B. 5 working days
    C. 10 working days   D. 30 calendar days

5. Which of the following is most commonly used as a venipuncture site?

    A. Middle forearm
    B. Antecubital area of the arm
    C. Dorsal side of the wrist
    D. Base of the thumb

6. Which of the following are common sites for the bleeding time test?
    I. Earlobe
    II. Heel
    III. Forearm
    IV. Finger

    The CORRECT answer is:

    A. I, III   B. II, IV   C. I, IV   D. II, III

7. Human cells contain _____ chromosomes each.

    A. 26   B. 46   C. 64   D. 72

8. Nongranular white blood cells are produced in

   A. the spleen
   B. bone marrow
   C. the liver
   D. all lymphatic tissue

9. For ABG analysis, the preferred site for blood collection is the _____ artery.

   A. radial
   B. subclavian
   C. popliteal
   D. femoral

10. Which of the following drugs may interfere with the results of a bleeding time test, even if it is ingested up to 7 to 10 days prior to testing?

    A. Acetaminophen
    B. Ethyl alcohol
    C. Aspirin
    D. Erythromycin

11. For which of the following would a butterfly needle be most beneficial?

    A. Burn patients
    B. Geriatric patients
    C. Heel punctures
    D. Newborn patients

12. When collecting a specimen for a blood culture, at least _____ ml of blood should be obtained in each collection

    A. 3
    B. 5
    C. 10
    D. 15

13. Which of the following is a skin puncture site?

    A. Ankle
    B. Heel
    C. Neck
    D. Wrist

14. When performing a blood culture on a pediatric patient younger than 10 years old, a rule of thumb is to collect

    A. 2 ml of blood, regardless of age or weight
    B. 1 ml of blood for each 10 pounds of the patient's weight
    C. 1 ml of blood each hour, over a 10-hour period
    D. 1 ml of blood for each year of the patient's age

15. The death of a segment of tissue, resulting from a lack of blood supply to that area, is known as a(n)

    A. edema
    B. necrosis
    C. infarct
    D. lysis

16. Which of the following is NOT a commonly occuring complication associated with the use of long-term indwelling lines in blood collection?

    A. Development of fibrin sheath over catheter tip
    B. Development of sclerosis
    C. Hemoconcentration
    D. Phlebitis

17. Under federal regulations, a laboratory certified to perform moderate complexity testing may conduct each of the following procedures EXCEPT

    A. throat culture screens
    B. quantitative semen analysis
    C. microscopic urinalysis
    D. urethral Gram's stain

18. During the bleeding time test, it is common practice to wick the blood at intervals of _____ until blood no longer stains the collection paper.

    A. 5 seconds
    B. 10 seconds
    C. 30 seconds
    D. 1 minute

19. The PT test is useful for

    A. evaluating platelet production
    B. detecting sickle cell disease
    C. supporting a diagnosis of anemia
    D. evaluating extrinsic coagulation

20. In general, glucose levels in a patient undergoing a glucose tolerance test should return to normal within _____ hour(s) after ingestion of the glucose drink.

    A. 1
    B. 2
    C. 3
    D. 4

21. Which of the following types of infection would require enteric isolation?

    A. Salmonella
    B. Whooping cough
    C. Shigella
    D. Tuberculosis

22. During the time that a glucose tolerance test is being performed,

    A. the patient should be encouraged to drink plenty of water
    B. a fasting blood collection is performed after a standard amount of glucose drink is given
    C. the patient's specimens should be timed from the fasting collection
    D. the patient may be allowed to chew sugarless gum

23. It is generally recommended that outpatients should be seated for about _____ before a venipuncture is attempted, in order to reduce the stress that might cause elevated levels in some tests.

    A. 15 minutes
    B. 30 minutes
    C. 1 hour
    D. 2 hours

24. The abbreviation *SOB*, appearing in a medical record, denotes

    A. subacute bacterial endocarditis
    B. a difficult patient
    C. shortness of breath
    D. elevated serum level

25. Laboratory analysis of a blood specimen, collected into an evacuated system with an EDTA additive, reveals a false low hematocrit. The most likely cause is

    A. excess additive due to short draw
    B. insufficient centrifugal force
    C. insufficient mixing of additive with specimen
    D. the use of an angle-head centrifuge

KEY (CORRECT ANSWERS)

1.	C	11.	B
2.	A	12.	C
3.	C	13.	B
4.	C	14.	D
5.	B	15.	C
6.	A	16.	C
7.	B	17.	B
8.	D	18.	C
9.	A	19.	D
10.	C	20.	B

21. A
22. A
23. A
24. C
25. A

TEST 2

DIRECTIONS: Each question or incomplete statement is followed by several suggested answers or completions. Select the one that BEST answers the question or completes the statement. *PRINT THE LETTER OF THE CORRECT ANSWER IN THE SPACE AT THE RIGHT.*

1. If a patient does not fast prior to a blood collection procedure, which of the following laboratory results is most likely to be affected?   1.____

   A. AST and CPK
   B. WBC
   C. Prothrombin time
   D. Triglycerides

2. In order to achieve an appropriate Westergren sedimentation rate in the analysis of blood specimens, it is necessary to use a tube that will give a ratio of citrate to blood volume that is about   2.____

   A. 1:1   B. 1:2   C. 1:4   D. 1:10

3. Each of the following may result in the failure to draw blood during a venipuncture EXCEPT the   3.____

   A. insertion of the needle through the vein
   B. loss of tube vacuum
   C. puncture of a sclerotic vein
   D. tying of a tourniquet too tightly

4. Which of the following tests requires a minimum draw of 10 ml of blood?   4.____

   A. Hepatitis C Ab
   B. HIV antigen
   C. APTT
   D. LDL cholesterol

5. The life span of a typical thrombocyte ranges from   5.____

   A. 9 to 12 days
   B. 1 day to 1 year
   C. 100 to 120 days
   D. 140 to 200 days

6. Which of the following tests requires the largest blood draw volume?   6.____

   A. Platelet function profile
   B. Catecholamines
   C. Drug screen
   D. Antibody titer

7. The preferred site for a heel stick is   7.____

   A. a previous puncture site
   B. the anteromedial aspect
   C. the medial or lateral aspect
   D. the posterior curve

8. Errors in blood smear procedures are typically due to each of the following EXCEPT   8.____

   A. too small a sample
   B. too long a delay in making the smear
   C. using a chipped slide
   D. too large a drop

9. Which of the following terms is used to describe blood that contains an abnormal amount of fatty substance?

   A. Adiposal
   B. Oleaginous
   C. Sclerotic
   D. Lipemic

10. Which of the following procedures is most commonly used by phlebotomists to increase the blood flow from a skin puncture site?

    A. Puncturing a site adjacent to the first puncture site
    B. Heating the area with a heating pad
    C. Squeezing the punctured finger
    D. Massaging the area

11. The _____ may be prevented by the practice of autologous transfusion.

    A. formation of antibodies
    B. development of diabetes mellitus
    C. development of polycythemia
    D. formation of antigens

12. The preferred angle for a finger stick is about _____ away from the longitudinal axis of the phalangeal bone.

    A. 10-20   B. 15-30   C. 45-60   D. 70-90

13. Which of the following analytes is LEAST likely to be affected by a patient's emotional stress?

    A. White blood count
    B. Red blood count
    C. Cortisol
    D. Serum iron

14. On what type of specimen is an occult blood analysis frequently performed?

    A. Synovial fluid
    B. Stool
    C. CSF
    D. Throat culture

15. Platelets are removed from the blood in the

    A. liver
    B. spleen
    C. lymphatic tissue
    D. bone marrow

16. Which of the following laboratory tests is used to detect hepatic disease?

    A. Fibrin degradation products
    B. Alanine aminotransferase (ALT/SGPT)
    C. Blood urea nitrogen (BUN)
    D. Acid phosphatase

17. In general, normal bleeding times for patients fall in the range of _____ minutes.

    A. 1 to 4   B. 2 to 8   C. 12 to 15   D. 15 to 30

18. The C-reactive protein test is used to

    A. screen for diabetes mellitus
    B. diagnose pancreatitis
    C. detect parathyroid and kidney disease
    D. detect inflammation

19. What is the term for objects that can harbor infectious agents and transmit infection?

    A. Fomites   B. Antigens   C. Hosts   D. Vectors

20. Which of the following is the proper procedure for filling a capillary or microcollection tube during skin puncture?

    A. Position the tube so that droplets will fall directly into the tube
    B. Use a syringe
    C. Allow the tube to fill by means of capillary action
    D. Use suction to pull blood into the tube

21. Which of the following is NOT an element of primary hemostasis?

    A. Formation of thromboplastin
    B. Activation of coagulation factors
    C. Constriction of blood vessels
    D. Aggregation of platelets

22. Each of the following items is necessary for an arterial puncture for the determination of ABG EXCEPT

    A. lidocaine   B. a tourniquet
    C. a syringe   D. heparin

23. Specimens of whole blood are typically collected in tubes with stoppers of each of the following colors EXCEPT

    A. green   B. lavender
    C. royal blue   D. yellow

24. Which of the following anticoagulants does NOT remove calcium through the formation of insoluble calcium salts?

    A. Ammonium oxalate   B. Sodium heparin
    C. Sodium citrate   D. EDTA

25. What is the term for a temporary deficiency of blood to a localized area, caused by an obstruction?

    A. Lysis   B. Ischemia
    C. Thrombosis   D. Infarction

4 (#2)

KEY (CORRECT ANSWERS)

1.	D		11.	A
2.	C		12.	A
3.	D		13.	B
4.	D		14.	B
5.	A		15.	B
6.	B		16.	B
7.	C		17.	B
8.	A		18.	D
9.	D		19.	A
10.	D		20.	C

21. A
22. B
23. C
24. B
25. B

EXAMINATION SECTION
TEST 1

DIRECTIONS: Each question or incomplete statement is followed by several suggested answers or completions. Select the one that BEST answers the question or completes the statement. *PRINT THE LETTER OF THE CORRECT ANSWER IN THE SPACE AT THE RIGHT.*

Questions 1-8.

DIRECTIONS: Questions 1 through 8 refer to the figure at the right, a diagram of the arteries in the leg. Place the letter that corresponds to each diagrammed artery in the space at the right.

1. Peroneal

2. Popliteal

3. Dorsalis pedis

4. Deep femoral

5. Anterior tibial

6. Plantar arch

7. Posterior tibial

8. Femoral

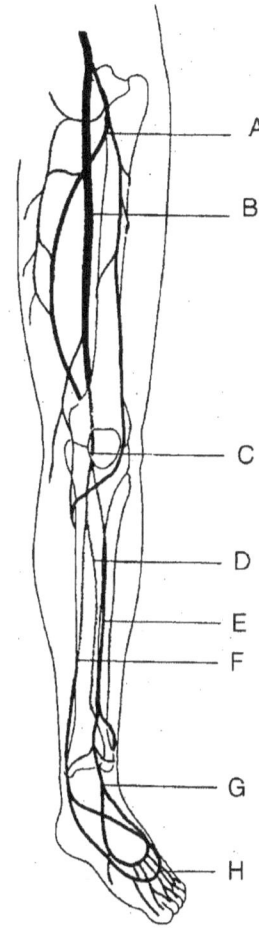

1.____

2.____

3.____

4.____

5.____

6.____

7.____

8.____

9. Which of the following infections would typically allow a phlebotomist to work, but without patient contact?

    A. Hepatitis B   B. Mononucleosis
    C. Herpes zoster   D. Hepatitis C

9.____

10. Process components of quality in specimen collection include each of the following EXCEPT

    A. hematomas
    B. use of correct anticoagulants
    C. expiration dates
    D. documentation procedures

11. Which of the following is a GTI infection?

    A. Gram-positive rods
    B. Streptococcus pyogenes
    C. coli
    D. Candida albicans

12. Each of the following is commonly used as a point of insertion for a central venous catheter (CVC) EXCEPT the

    A. superior vena cava at or above the junction of the right atrium
    B. subclavian vein
    C. cephalic vein
    D. jugular vein

13. Under federal regulations, which of the following levels of laboratory testing requires a minimum requirement of a high school diploma (or equivalent) for practitioners?

    A. Waived testing
    B. Practitioner-performed microscopy
    C. Moderate complexity testing
    D. High complexity testing

14. Each of the following is recommended during a venipuncture procedure EXCEPT

    A. inserting the needle in a direct line with the vein
    B. if a syringe is used, retracting the plunger slowly and gradually
    C. turning the needle so that the bevel is in a downward position
    D. if an evacuated tube is used, pushing the tube forward as far as it will go after the needle is inserted

15. Which of the following conditions is frequently accompanied by ketosis?

    A. Diabetes mellitus
    B. Hyperthyroidism
    C. Liver disease
    D. Bacterial infection

16. A blood collection vacuum tube that is 10.25 mm wide and 82 mm long has a draw volume of _____ ml.

    A. 2.0   B. 4.0   C. 6.0   D. 10.0

17. Which of the following tests are measured through blood coagulation monitoring by point-of-care testing?
    I. pH
    II. PT
    III. APTT
    IV. pCO_2

    The CORRECT answer is:

    A. I only   B. I, IV   C. II, III   D. III, IV

18. What is the maximum amount of blood (ml) that may be drawn at any one time from a pediatric patient who weighs 77 pounds? 18.____

   A. 5   B. 10   C. 20   D. 30

19. Which of the following federal agencies evaluates the safety, clinical effectiveness, and medical effectiveness of the equipment and supplies used in blood collection? 19.____

   A. AMA   B. CDC   C. FDA   D. OSHA

20. If laboratory analysis of blood specimens produces false high BUN values, the most likely cause is 20.____

   A. sodium heparin salt interference
   B. ammonium heparin salt interference
   C. cell distortion or hemolysis
   D. a short draw

21. Typically, blood collection procedures on a hospitalized child should be performed 21.____

   A. in the child's bed
   B. in the presence of other children
   C. beside the child's bed, with the child standing or in a chair
   D. in the treatment room

22. Which of the following is a tubular instrument that is used in patients with kidney disease to gain access to venous blood? 22.____

   A. Catheter   B. Cannula
   C. Heparin lock   D. Fistula

23. What is the legal term for the administration of care in an unprofessional or unskillful way? 23.____

   A. Battery   B. Negligence
   C. Malpractice   D. Misfeasance

24. Ideally, an ABC specimen should be analyzed within _____ of its collection. 24.____

   A. 10 minutes   B. 45 minutes
   C. 2 hours   D. 4 hours

25. Under federal regulations, practitioner-performed microscopy may NOT involve 25.____

   A. fern tests
   B. urine sedimentation examinations
   C. Gram's stains
   D. pinworm examinations

KEY (CORRECT ANSWERS)

1.	F	11.	D
2.	C	12.	C
3.	G	13.	C
4.	A	14.	C
5.	E	15.	A
6.	H	16.	B
7.	D	17.	C
8.	B	18.	D
9.	C	19.	C
10.	C	20.	B

21. D
22. B
23. C
24. A
25. C

TEST 2

DIRECTIONS: Each question or incomplete statement is followed by several suggested answers or completions. Select the one that BEST answers the question or completes the statement. *PRINT THE LETTER OF THE CORRECT ANSWER IN THE SPACE AT THE RIGHT.*

1. Which of the following anticoagulants works by inhibiting thrombin?   1.____

    A. Lithium oxalate B. Sodium heparin
    C. EDTA D. SPS

2. Leakproof containers used in health care workplaces for the reception of biohazardous waste are typically color-coded   2.____

    A. orange B. blue C. green D. red

3. Which of the following needle gauges are typically used for the collection of donor units?   3.____
    I. 16
    II. 18
    III. 21
    IV. 25
   The CORRECT answer is:

    A. I *only* B. I, II
    C. III, IV D. II, III, IV

4. _____ blood _____ levels cause insulin to be released into the bloodstream.   4.____

    A. Decreased; cholesterol B. Increased; cholesterol
    C. Decreased; glucose D. Increased; glucose

5. Which of the following is a clinical immunology procedure?   5.____

    A. Hemosiderin B. ASO titer
    C. Hematocrit D. ABO grouping

6. The primary goal of standard precautions in a health care setting is to   6.____

    A. prevent the spread of infections through direct or indirect contact
    B. control nosocomial infections
    C. limit the organization's legal liability in case of an accident
    D. prevent the spread of blood-borne pathogens

7. Which of the following terms is used to denote the dissolution of a red blood cell?   7.____

    A. Lysis B. Septicemia
    C. Ischemia D. Cyanosis

8. Quality control standards in most health care facilities state that an evacuated tube that does not contain ± _____ % of the labeled blood draw should be considered defective.   8.____

    A. 1 B. 5 C. 10 D. 20

9. Which of the following federal agencies is responsible for formulating the rules concerning exposure to blood-borne pathogens?   9.____

    A. OSHA B. JCAHO C. CDC D. HCFA

10. Which of the following types of blood cells typically stain orange-red with acidic dyes?

    A. Basophils
    B. Eosinophils
    C. Monocytes
    D. Neutrophils

11. Which of the following cumulative trauma disorders occurs most commonly among phlebotomists?

    A. Carpal tunnel syndrome
    B. Tendonitis
    C. Trigger finger
    D. Back disorders

12. If each of the following draws is to be performed during a single venipuncture, and an evacuated system is used, which should be performed LAST? _____ containing tubes.

    A. Citrate
    B. EDTA
    C. Fluoride
    D. Heparin

13. Which of the following is NOT measured by a blood gas analysis?

    A. Na^+
    B. pCO_2
    C. pO_2
    D. pH

14. In anatomic descriptions of the body, which of the following planes runs lengthwise from front to back and divides the body into its right and left halves?

    A. Dorsal
    B. Medial
    C. Sagittal
    D. Transverse

15. In which of the following gauges are butterfly needles typically not available?

    A. 18
    B. 21
    C. 23
    D. 25

16. The most commonly contracted type of nosocomial infections involve

    A. ears or throat
    B. surgical wounds
    C. the urinary tract
    D. the respiratory tract

17. Which of the following tests requires a minimum of 5 ml of blood?

    A. PSA
    B. von Willebrand's factor assay
    C. Catecholamines
    D. ABG

18. What is the legal term for a procedure in which written questions are sent to a witness in a lawsuit who makes a reply under oath?

    A. Interrogatory
    B. Demand-letter
    C. Deposition
    D. Discovery

19. Which of the following is a blood metabolite?

    A. Water
    B. Lipid
    C. Globulin
    D. Chloride

20. Which of the following specimens is obtained from the abdominal cavity?

    A. Synovial fluid
    B. CSF
    C. Lymph
    D. Peritoneal fluid

21. Specimens for testing _____ may require warming for transport and handling.   21._____

    A. bilirubin   B. carotene
    C. cryofibrinogen   D. parathyroid hormone

22. To detect an infection, a _____ urine specimen is preferred.   22._____

    A. random   B. 24-hour
    C. clean catch   D. routine

23. The serum of a collected blood specimen appears very dark red. This is most likely a sign that   23._____

    A. clotting is incomplete
    B. hemolysis has occurred
    C. the specimen has not been adequately mixed with the additive
    D. a short draw has been collected

24. During testing of whole blood specimens, it is noted that an incomplete barrier is forming within the sample.   24._____
    The most likely cause is

    A. insufficient mixing of additive with specimen
    B. insufficient centrifugal force
    C. the vacuum is too high
    D. incorrect additive

25. Which of the following are tests used to assess secondary hemostatic processes?   25._____
    I. PT
    II. Platelet count
    III. APTT
    IV. Bleeding time
    The CORRECT answer is:

    A. I, IV   B. I, III   C. II, IV   D. II, III

KEY (CORRECT ANSWERS)

1.	B	11.	B
2.	D	12.	C
3.	B	13.	A
4.	D	14.	C
5.	B	15.	A
6.	B	16.	C
7.	A	17.	B
8.	C	18.	A
9.	A	19.	B
10.	B	20.	D

21. C
22. C
23. B
24. B
25. C

HEMATOLOGY
EXAMINATION SECTION

TEST 1

DIRECTIONS: Each question or incomplete statement is followed by several suggested answers or completions. Select the one that BEST answers the question or completes the statement. *PRINT THE LETTER OF THE CORRECT ANSWER IN THE SPACE AT THE RIGHT.*

1. Which of the following animal parasites CANNOT be present in a blood smear? 1.____
   - A. Plasmodium
   - B. Anopheles
   - C. Trypanosoma
   - D. Schistosoma

2. Pernicious anemia is caused by a deficiency of vitamin 2.____
   - A. K
   - B. B_{12}
   - C. D
   - D. A

3. Another vitamin deficiency that is similar to pernicious anemia in that it presents with anemia, macrocytic r.b.c., and megaloblasts in the marrow is _____ deficiency. 3.____
   - A. folic acid
   - B. vitamin D
   - C. vitamin B_2
   - D. vitamin K

4. In typhus, brucellosis, tuberculosis, and monocytic leukemia, you would expect the monocytes to be 4.____
   - A. increased
   - B. decreased
   - C. normal in number
   - D. either increased or decreased

5. In mumps, whooping cough, and infectious mononucleosis, you would expect the lymphocytes to be 5.____
   - A. increased
   - B. decreased
   - C. normal in number
   - D. either increased or decreased

6. A neutrophilic leukocytosis with *shift to the left* occurs in 6.____
   - A. radiation sickness
   - B. viral hepatitis
   - C. leukemia
   - D. appendicitis

7. In appendicitis, meningitis, diphtheria, pneumonia, and leukemia, you would expect the total white cell count to be 7.____
   - A. increased
   - B. decreased
   - C. normal
   - D. increased or decreased

8. The percent number of monocytes is INCREASED in
    I. whooping cough
    II. tuberculosis
    III. typhus fever
    IV. hay fever
   The CORRECT answer is:

   A. I, II B. II, III C. III, IV D. I, IV

9. In typhoid fever, influenza, measles, brucellosis, and neutropenia, you would expect the total white cell count to be

   A. increased
   C. normal
   B. decreased
   D. increased or decreased

10. The percent number of lymphocytes is INCREASED in
    I. whooping cough
    II. tuberculosis
    III. scarlet fever
    IV. infectious mononucleosis
    The CORRECT answer is:

    A. I only
    C. I, IV
    B. II, III, IV
    D. I, II, III, IV

11. Atypical lymphocytes are seen in the following conditions:

    A. Toxoplasmosis
    C. Infectious hepatitis
    B. Cytomegalovirus infection
    D. All of the above

12. A macrocytosis characteristically occurs in

    A. sickle cell anemia
    C. lead poisoning
    B. Tay-Sachs disease
    D. pernicious anemia

13. With a normal rate of red cell production in a newborn infant, the following percentage of circulating r.b.c. is reticulocytes:

    A. 0.5 - 1.0%
    C. 2.0 - 6.0%
    B. 1.0 - 2.0%
    D. 6.0 - 7.5%

14. In a normal bone marrow smear, you would expect to find the following number of reticulocytes:

    A. 0 - 1.0%
    C. 5 - 15.0%
    B. 1 - 5.0%
    D. 15 - 35.0%

15. In a normal bone marrow smear, you would expect to find the following number of lymphocytes:

    A. 0 - 3.0%
    C. 4 - 16.0%
    B. 3 - 11.3%
    D. 20 - 27.5%

16. In a normal bone marrow smear, you would expect to find the following number of plasma cells:

    A. 0 - 1.0%
    C. 1.5 - 2.0%
    B. 1.0 - 1.5%
    D. 2.0 - 2.5%

17. In a normal bone marrow smear, you would expect to find the following number of normo- 17.____
    blasts:

    A. 0 - 5.0% B. 1 - 2.0%
    C. 2 - 5.0% D. 5 - 20.0%

18. In a normal bone marrow smear, you would expect to find the following number of myelo- 18.____
    blasts:

    A. 0 - 5.0% B. 5 - 10.0%
    C. 10 - 15.0% D. 15 - 20.0%

19. In a normal bone marrow smear, you would expect to find the following number of neutro- 19.____
    philic myelocytes:

    A. 0 - 2.5% B. 2.5 - 5.0%
    C. 5 - 20.0% D. 20 - 29.8%

20. In a normal bone marrow smear, you would expect to find the following number of neutro- 20.____
    philic metamyelocytes:

    A. 0 - 1.0% B. 1 - 3.0%
    C. 3 - 4.0% D. 5 - 10.0%

21. In a normal bone marrow smear, you would expect to find the following number of neutro- 21.____
    philic band (stab) cells:

    A. 0 - 2.0% B. 2 - 5.0%
    C. 10 - 15.0% D. 15 - 35.0%

22. In a normal bone marrow smear, you would expect to find the following number of seg- 22.____
    mented neutrophils:

    A. 0 - 5.0% B. 7 - 30.0%
    C. 35 - 60.0% D. 60 - 96.0%

23. A consistently reliable means of differentiating between human and animal blood is the 23.____
    _____ test.

    A. Van Slyke B. Guaiac
    C. Teichmann's D. Precipitin

24. After ACTH injection, the circulating eosinophil count is normally 24.____

    A. increased B. decreased
    C. unaffected D. either A or B

25. The 0.85% solution of sodium chloride is known as 25.____

    A. Helly's fluid B. Zenker's fluid
    C. Bouin's fluid D. normal saline

KEY (CORRECT ANSWERS)

1. D
2. B
3. A
4. A
5. A

6. D
7. A
8. B
9. B
10. C

11. D
12. D
13. C
14. B
15. C

16. A
17. D
18. A
19. C
20. D

21. D
22. B
23. D
24. B
25. D

TEST 2

DIRECTIONS: Each question or incomplete statement is followed by several suggested answers or completions. Select the one that BEST answers the question or completes the statement. *PRINT THE LETTER OF THE CORRECT ANSWER IN THE SPACE AT THE RIGHT.*

1. Which of the following solutions may be employed as diluting fluids for a red cell count? 1.____

    A. Hayem's solution
    B. 3% acetic acid
    C. Hydrochloric acid
    D. Zenker's fluid

2. The TOTAL ruled area of the counting chamber covers _____ sq.mm. 2.____

    A. 3 B. 9 C. 18 D. 27

3. The dilution range of a red cell pipette is 3.____

    A. 1:10 - 1:100
    B. 1:20 - 1:200
    C. 1:50 - 1:500
    D. 1:100 - 1:1,000

4. The dilution range of a white cell pipette is 4.____

    A. 1:10 - 1:100
    B. 1:20 - 1:200
    C. 1:50 - 1:500
    D. 1:100 - 1:1,000

5. In routing RBC, the red cells are counted under high power in the following number of smallest squares: 5.____

    A. 24 B. 32 C. 64 D. 80

6. An RBC should be replated whenever the greatest variation between *R* squares EXCEEDS _____ cells. 6.____

    A. 5 B. 20 C. 50 D. 75

7. For routine RBC, the blood is diluted 1:200 and, in order to report r.b.c./cu.mm., the number of these cells counted in 80 of the smallest squares may be directly multiplied by 7.____

    A. 50 B. 100 C. 1000 D. 10,000

8. In routine WBC, the white cells are counted under low power in the following number of sq. mm.: 8.____

    A. 1 B. 2 C. 3 D. 4

9. A WBC should be replated whenever the greatest variation between *W* squares EXCEEDS _____ cells. 9.____

    A. 4 B. 6 C. 8 D. 12

10. For routine WBC, the blood is diluted 1:20 and, in order to report w.b.c. per cu. mm., the number of these cells counted within 4 sq. mm. may be directly multiplied by 10.____

    A. 50 B. 100 C. 1,000 D. 10,000

11. Which of the following tests ALWAYS require blood drawn from a vein?

    A. Capillary fragility
    B. Lee & White
    C. Ivy bleeding time
    D. Fonio's thrombocyte count

12. Which of the following tests does NOT call for dilution of blood in a special diluting pipette?

    A. Total erythrocyte count
    B. Total leukocyte count
    C. Sedimentation rate
    D. Circulating eosinophil count

13. Which of the following tests does NOT require the preparation of a blood smear?

    A. Reticulocyte count
    B. Sedimentation rate
    C. Direct Coombs
    D. Mean corpuscular diameter

14. The hemoglobin concentration of blood may be INCREASED in:
    I. Anemia
    II. Polycythemia vera
    III. Dehydration
    IV. Pernicious anemia
    The CORRECT answer is:

    A. I, IV
    B. II, III
    C. II, III, IV
    D. III, IV

15. The total body hemoglobin is INCREASED in:
    I. Anemia
    II. Polycythemia vera
    III. Dehydration
    IV. Erythremia secondary to severe pulmonary disease or congenital heart disease
    The CORRECT answer is:

    A. II only
    B. II, III, IV
    C. II, IV
    D. I, II

16. In a case of obstructive jaundice, you would expect the erythrocyte fragility to be

    A. increased
    B. decreased
    C. normal
    D. either A or B

17. In a case of hereditary spherocytosis, you would expect the erythrocyte fragility to be

    A. increased
    B. decreased
    C. normal
    D. either A or B

18. In cases of sickle cell anemia, the red cells become sickle-shaped when

    A. oxygen is added to the cells
    B. oxygen is removed from the cells
    C. cell fragility is increased
    D. cell fragility is decreased

19. In disseminated intravascular coagulation, the following coagulation components are frequently depleted: 19._____

    A. Platelets
    B. Factor VIII
    C. Factor II
    D. All of the above

20. Hypochromia is seen in   20._____

    A. iron deficiency anemia
    B. thallasemia
    C. the anemia of chronic disease
    D. all of the above

21. Heinz bodies occur in r.b.c. in which of the following conditions?   21._____
    I. Drug-induced hemolysis
    II. Hemolysis associated with the unstable hemoglobins
    III. Hemolysis associated with hereditary deficiency of glucose-6-phosphate dehydrogenase
    IV. PKT

    The CORRECT answer is:

    A. II only
    B. II, III
    C. I, II, III
    D. I, II, III, IV

22. The counting chamber has the following depth: _____ mm.   22._____

    A. 0.05   B. 0.10   C. 0.15   D. 0.20

23. The counting chamber has a depth of 1/10 mm. and a total ruled area which measures 3 mm. on each side.   23._____
    Therefore, the counting area of a chamber has a ruled area of 9 sq. mm., a depth of 0.1 mm., and a volume of _____ cu. mm.

    A. 0.3   B. 0.9   C. 1.2   D. 1.5

24. Each of the smallest squares of the hemocytometer grating measures _____ sq. mm.   24._____

    A. 1   B. 1/4   C. 1/40   D. 1/400

25. The so-called *direct method* of thrombocyte enumeration requires a   25._____

    A. dilution of blood in a red pipette using a special (such as Rees-Ecker) fluid
    B. blood smear
    C. both A and B
    D. neither A nor B

KEY (CORRECT ANSWERS)

1.	A	11.	B
2.	B	12.	C
3.	D	13.	B
4.	A	14.	B
5.	D	15.	C
6.	B	16.	B
7.	D	17.	A
8.	D	18.	B
9.	D	19.	D
10.	A	20.	C

21. C
22. B
23. B
24. D
25. A

TEST 3

DIRECTIONS: Each question or incomplete statement is followed by several suggested answers or completions. Select the one that BEST answers the question or completes the statement. *PRINT THE LETTER OF THE CORRECT ANSWER IN THE SPACE AT THE RIGHT.*

1. To remove fresh blood from a lab coat, you would apply   1.____

    A. a 3% hydrogen peroxide solution, then rinse thoroughly with water
    B. methyl alcohol
    C. a 10% solution of sodium carbonate
    D. a solvent such as benzene or chloroform

2. Which of the following achromatic objectives would be an oil immersion objective? N.A.   2.____

    A. 0.35   B. 0.65   C. 0.85   D. 1.25

3. The abnormal variation in shape among r.b.c. is called   3.____

    A. anisocytosis   B. poikilocytosis
    C. polychromatophilia   D. spherocytosis

4. The abnormal variation in size among r.b.c. is called   4.____

    A. anisocytosis   B. poikilocytosis
    C. polychromatophilia   D. spherocytosis

5. Polychromatophilia is also called   5.____

    A. poikilocytosis   B. polychromasia
    C. erythroblastosis   D. neutrophilia

6. *Juveniles* are technically known as   6.____

    A. myelocytes   B. metamyelocytes
    C. microcytes   D. segmented cells

7. Which of the following cells is NOT a member of the granulocytic series?   7.____

    A. Basophil   B. Monocyte
    C. Eosinophil   D. Neutrophil

8. Which of the following cells is characterized by a number of bluish-black coarse cytoplasmic granules?   8.____

    A. Monoblast   B. Neutrophil
    C. Eosinophil   D. Basophil

9. Which of the following cells is characterized by numerous large brilliant red cytoplasmic granules?   9.____

    A. Basophil   B. Neutrophil
    C. Eosinophil   D. Monocyte

10. Which of the following cells of the granulocytic series is characterized by a bean- or kidney-shaped nucleus?

    A. Myelocyte
    B. Metamyelocyte
    C. Basophil
    D. Segmented cell

11. Which of the following tests would NOT be included in a routine CBC? _____ count.

    A. Differential leukocyte
    B. Total erythrocyte
    C. Reticulocyte
    D. Total leukocyte

12. The test which determines the circulating eosinophils before and four hours after treatment with ACTH is the _____ test.

    A. Widal
    B. Lee & White
    C. Ascoli
    D. Thorn

13. The IMMEDIATE precursor of the thrombocyte is

    A. Promegakaryocyte
    B. Megakaryocyte
    C. Megakaryoblast
    D. Embryoblast

14. With a normal rate of red cell production in adults, the following percentage of circulating r.b.c. are reticulocytes:

    A. 0 - 0.5%
    B. 0.5 - 1.0%
    C. 1.5 - 2.0%
    D. 2.0 - 2.5%

15. The NORMAL adult female values for the red cell count (RBC) are _____ millions/cu. mm.

    A. 2.5 - 3.3
    B. 3.4 - 4.2
    C. 4.3 - 5.5
    D. 5.5 - 6.6

16. The NORMAL range of erythrocyte count (RBC) in adult males is _____ millions/cu. mm.

    A. 3.0 - 4.0
    B. 4.0 - 4.5
    C. 4.5 - 6.0
    D. 6.0 - 8.8

17. The NORMAL range of PCV in adult males is

    A. 33 - 38%
    B. 40 - 44%
    C. 45 - 49%
    D. 50 - 56%

18. The NORMAL range of MCH is

    A. 28-32 micromicrograms
    B. 33 - 38%
    C. 1.7 - 2.5 microns
    D. 80-94 cu. microns

19. The NORMAL range of MCV is

    A. 28-32 micromicrograms
    B. 80 - 94 cu. microns
    C. 33 - 38%
    D. 1.8 - 2.3 microns

20. The NORMAL number of grams of hemoglobin in an adult female is _____ plus or minus 2 grams%.

    A. 10
    B. 12
    C. 14
    D. 16

21. The dilution correction factor for ordinary red cell counts (RBC) is   21.____
    A. 100   B. 125   C. 150   D. 200

22. Which of the following blood dilutions is employed for routine RBC?   22.____
    A. 1:10   B. 1:50   C. 1:100   D. 1:200

23. Which of the following blood dilutions is employed for routine WBC?   23.____
    A. 1:10   B. 1:20   C. 1:30   D. 1:100

24. When you draw blood to the 1.0 mark of an RBC pipette and platelet diluting fluid to the 101 mark, you have the following blood dilution: 24.____
    A. 1:20   B. 1:50   C. 1:100   D. 1:200

25. When you draw blood to the 1.0 mark of a WBC pipette and white cell diluting fluid to the 11.0 mark, you have the following blood dilution: 25.____
    A. 1:10   B. 1:20   C. 1:100   D. 1:200

KEY (CORRECT ANSWERS)

1. A		11. C	
2. D		12. D	
3. B		13. B	
4. A		14. B	
5. B		15. C	
6. B		16. C	
7. B		17. C	
8. D		18. A	
9. C		19. B	
10. B		20. C	

21. D
22. D
23. B
24. C
25. A

EXAMINATION SECTION
TEST 1

DIRECTIONS: Each question or incomplete statement is followed by several suggested answers or completions. Select the one that BEST answers the question or completes the statement. *PRINT THE LETTER OF THE CORRECT ANSWER IN THE SPACE AT THE RIGHT.*

Questions 1-15.   **BLOOD BANKING**

DIRECTIONS: Questions 1 through 15 are to be answered on the basis of blood banking.

1. Rouleaux formation may be distinguished for agglutination by the addition of which one of the following substances?

    A. Saline
    B. Fibrinogen
    C. Plasma from a subject
    D. Dextran

    1.____

2. Which one of the following components is NOT known to exhibit hemolysis, *in vitro*, or agglutination at 4C°? Anti-

    A. A_1
    B. Le^a in presence of complement
    C. I
    D. Kell

    2.____

3. Which one of the following antigens or antibodies NEVER requires the antiglobulin reaction?
    Determination of

    A. Kell antigen or red cells
    B. anti-e
    C. anti-P
    D. Rh variant (Du)

    3.____

4. Which one of the following types of antibodies in the mother is NOT significant in neonatal hemolysis of the infant?

    A. Anti-Kell
    B. Hemolytic Anti-A
    C. IgM Antibodies
    D. IgG Antibodies

    4.____

5. Which one of the following is NORMALLY found in the plasma of ABH non-secretors?

    A. Le^a substance
    B. Anti-i
    C. Rh antigen
    D. A_2 substance

    5.____

6. Which one of the following is an ACCEPTABLE procedure for detecting weak antibodies by concentration?

    A. Dialysis
    B. Centrifugation at 3000 RPM for 30 minutes
    C. Diminution of Albumin
    D. Boiling

    6.____

7. Which one of the following conditions or procedures may cause ABO grouping error?

   A. Using a mixture of A_1 and A_2 cells for reverse typing
   B. Warming the ABO test
   C. Presence of anti-H in serum
   D. Working in a hot room at $150°C$

8. A Group A_2B patient without detectable anti-A_1 CANNOT be transfused with whole boood from a donor who has

   A. A_1 red cells
   B. anti-A_1 antibody in his serum detectable at $4°C$ and $37°C$
   C. group O red cells and high titer hemolytic anti-B in his serum
   D. B red cells

9. Paternity can be excluded if the mother is group B and M, the alleged father is group 0 and N, and the child is group

   A. O   B. A   C. B   D. MN

10. A delayed hemolytic transfusion reaction is associated with which one of the following?

    A. A previously transfused patient who is Fy^a negative and who is given Fya positive red cells
    B. Strong cold antibody
    C. Transfusions of ABO incompatible blood
    D. Transfusion of whole blood to a patient with antibodies to leukocytes

11. Positive identification of blood specimens is important in all clinical laboratories. This is especially important in blood banking because a simple error may have a direct fatal outcome.
    If a recipient specimen arrives unlabeled in the blood bank, the MOST appropriate course of action for the technician to take is to

    A. quickly label the specimen
    B. ask the floor nurse to send the label to the blood bank for attachment to the tube
    C. discard the specimen and request a new, properly labeled specimen
    D. ask the attending physician to countersign a label prepared by the floor clerk

12. Blood anticoagulated with heparin ALONE must be transfused within

    A. 6 hours   B. 24 hours   C. 48 hours   D. 21 days

13. A bag of blood which has been opened under sterile conditions should NOT be transfused after

    A. 6 hours   B. 24 hours   C. 48 hours   D. 21 days

14. Which one of the following conditions has the MOST serious effect on red cells stored in ACD in a blood bank refrigerator?

    A. Exposure to room temperature for 10 minutes
    B. Blood warming to $7°C$ for 10 minutes

C. Blood freezing at 2°C for 10 minutes
D. Blood inverted for 2 days

15. Which one of the following red cell antibodies is BEST detected by the antiglobulin technique?   15.____

    A. Naturally occurring anti-A
    B. Anti-Kell
    C. Anti-P
    D. Anti-he^a

Questions 16-30. **CLINICAL CHEMISTRY**

DIRECTIONS: Questions 16 through 30 are to be answered on the basis of clinical chemistry.

16. When mixing 50 ml of sulfuric acid with 950 ml water, it is IMPORTANT to   16.____

    A. stir the sulfuric acid before mixing
    B. stir the water before mixing
    C. pour the sulfuric acid carefully into the water
    D. pour the water carefully into the sulfuric acid

17. A water bath is maintained at a CONSTANT temperature by a   17.____

    A. thermometer   B. dehumidifier
    C. pressure gauge   D. thermoregulator

18. A centrifuge operates on the principle of   18.____

    A. humidity   B. velocity
    C. gravitational force   D. osmotic pressure

19. The pH of a 0.5N solution of sodium chloride is NEAREST to   19.____

    A. 6.0   B. 7.0   C. 7.5   D. 8.5

20. Which one of the following is NOT a carbohydrate?   20.____

    A. Starch   B. Fructose   C. Galactose   D. Glycine

21. Electrophoresis measures the   21.____

    A. ionic strength of a solution
    B. migration of proteins
    C. solubility product
    D. voltage of a solution

22. A wavelength of 6,000 Angstroms is the SAME as   22.____

    A. 6,000 millimicrons   B. 6 microns
    C. 600 nanometers   D. 6,000 nanometers

23. Assume that a technician accidentally gets a spray of sulfuric acid in his eye. He should IMMEDIATELY

    A. call the optometrist
    B. flush the eye with water
    C. wash the eye with boric acid
    D. put on his safety goggles

24. A solution containing a concentration of 100 mgs per deciliter is the SAME as

    A. 1 gram per liter
    B. 10 grams per liter
    C. 10 mgs per ml
    D. 1 gram per ml

25. The one of the following blood plasma values that is MARKEDLY abnormal is

    A. 85 mg% glucose
    B. 139 meq sodium
    C. 0.9 mg% creatinine
    D. 14.5 mg% uric acid

26. A blood plasma dialysate is obtained by

    A. removing the proteins from the plasma
    B. diluting the plasma with an equal volume of saline
    C. centrifuging the plasma at 3,000 rpm
    D. keeping the plasma in the refrigerator overnight

27. The purpose of the photocell in a flame photometer is to

    A. filter out the proteins
    B. remove dust particles
    C. multiply the electrical signal
    D. convert light energy to electrical energy

28. The Van Slyke apparatus is designed for the

    A. determination of blood gases
    B. analysis of electrolytes
    C. determination of creatinine
    D. determination of viscosity

29. A technician's determination shows that a patient has a very high blood glucose. He should IMMEDIATELY

    A. call the patient and give him the result
    B. call the result to the attention of the supervisor
    C. enter the result on the patient's chart
    D. disregard the result as a technical error

30. Titration of an acid with a base yields

    A. another acid
    B. another base
    C. a salt
    D. an alcohol

KEY (CORRECT ANSWERS)

1.	A	16.	C
2.	D	17.	D
3.	C	18.	C
4.	C	19.	B
5.	A	20.	D
6.	A	21.	B
7.	B	22.	C
8.	C	23.	B
9.	B	24.	A
10.	A	25.	D
11.	C	26.	A
12.	B	27.	D
13.	B	28.	A
14.	C	29.	B
15.	B	30.	C

TEST 2

DIRECTIONS: Each question or incomplete statement is followed by several suggested answers or completions. Select the one that BEST answers the question or completes the statement. *PRINT THE LETTER OF THE CORRECT ANSWER IN THE SPACE AT THE RIGHT.*

Questions 1-15. **HEMATOLOGY**

DIRECTIONS: Questions 1 through 15 are to be answered on the basis of hematology.

1. Coincidence correction becomes INCREASINGLY significant in the Coulter *R* System when the

    A. counts are low
    B. cells are large
    C. cells are small
    D. counts are high

2. Increased reticulocytosis is an INDICATION of

    A. marrow suppression
    B. an increase in younger red cells in peripheral blood
    C. early leukemia
    D. an increase in older red cells in peripheral blood

3. Spherocytes are MOST commonly found in the blood of persons with

    A. iron deficiency anemia
    B. acute monocytic leukemia
    C. sickle cell anemia
    D. congenital hemolytic anemia

4. Target cells are MOST commonly found in the blood of persons with

    A. megaloblastic anemia
    B. thalassemia
    C. anemia of chronic renal disease
    D. chronic lymphocytic leukemia

5. A positive Heinz test is NOT characteristic of

    A. protein denaturation in red cell
    B. hemolytic anemia
    C. megaloblastic anemia
    D. red cell glucose 6 phosphate dehydrogenase deficiency

6. When helmet-shaped red cells are observed on a smear of peripheral blood, they should be

    A. ignored
    B. noted because they denote sickle cell anemia
    C. reported because they may reflect a hemolytic anemia such as microangiopathic or red cell enzyme deficient hemolytic anemia
    D. reported because they are characteristic of acute leukemia

7. A patient with Factor VII deficiency is MOST likely to have an abnormal value when which one of the following tests is performed?

   A. Platelet count
   B. Clot retraction
   C. Partial thromboplastin time
   D. Prothrombin time

8. A patient is known to have a very low white blood cells count. GREATER accuracy for this patient can be obtained by using a dilution which

   A. is the same as for normal or high counts
   B. contains more blood and more diluent
   C. contains more blood and less diluent
   D. contains less blood and the same amount of diluent

9. A 1:20 dilution of blood is to be introduced into a white blood cell counting chamber of 0.1 mm depth. The white blood cell count is to be reported per cubic millimeter. To obtain the result, the total number of cells counted in four squares of .1 sq. mm. each should be multiplied by

   A. 20   B. 50   C. 100   D. 200

10. Which one of the following findings makes a donor of blood INELIGIBLE for transfusions?

    A. Hepatitis B antigen positive by CEP (counterelec-trophoresis) two years ago, but negative by radio-immune assay now
    B. *Green* plasma from a 30-year-old woman whose bili-rubin level is 0.6 mg%
    C. Hepatitis B antibody negative whenever tested
    D. Hematocrit 52%

11. Under emergency circumstances, type O red cells or even whole blood may be transfused to a type A, B, or AB recipient.
    Which one of the following situations would NOT preclude such a transfusion?

    A. Minor crossmatch is incompatible.
    B. Presence of strong hemolytic antibody to Type A and Type B
    C. Plasma of blood slated for transfusion is cloudy and shows hemolysis
    D. Whole blood with agglutinating titer of 1:256 for anti-A and 1:128 for anti-B

12. Which one of the following has the LOWEST percent standard deviation (variance) in a well-run clinical laboratory?

    A. Manual white blood cell count (WBC)
    B. Hemoglobin by cyanmethemoglobin method
    C. Phase platelet count
    D. Reticulocyte count

13. The hematocrit can be calculated if which one of the following is ACCURATELY known? Mean corpuscular

    A. hemoglobin concentration (MCHC) and mean corpuscular hemoglobin (MCH)
    B. hemoglobin (MCH) and hemoglobin (hgb)
    C. volume (MCV) and mean corpuscular hemoglobin concentration (MCHC)
    D. volume (MCV) and red blood cell count (RBC)

14. The Coulter R blood cell counter is based on the principle that it

   A. detects difference in color of stain from which red and white cell counts are calculated
   B. determines the optical density of each cell
   C. counts changes in electric resistance as cells in suspension pass
   D. senses the magnetic resonance of atomic nuclei

15. The reagents added to citrated test plasma for determination of partial thromboplastin time include

   A. calcium chloride, thromboplastin and normal plasma
   B. calcium chloride, platelet substitutes, and kaolin
   C. thromboplastin with added calcium chloride and kaolin
   D. barium sulfate absorbed normal plasma and M/40 calcium chloride

Questions 16-30.   **HISTOLOGY**

DIRECTIONS: Questons 16 through 30 are to be answered on the basis of histology.

16. The clearing agent that removes alcohol MOST rapidly following alcoholic dehydration of a tissue specimen is

   A. oil of cloves   B. toluene
   C. xylene   D. chloroform

17. Which of the following volumes of 95% alcohol should be used to prepare 1000 ml of 50% alcohol?
   _____ ml.

   A. 450   B. 475   C. 500   D. 525

18. All of the following dyes may be used to selectively stain lipids in tissue sections EXCEPT

   A. Nile blue   B. oil red O
   C. Cresyl violet   D. Sudan black

19. The technique LEAST likely to be used in a regressive staining procedure is

   A. overstaining   B. understaining
   C. destaining   D. differentiation

20. The number of 5 micron thick cross-sections obtained by serially sectioning a 1.35 cmlong segment of the jejunum is

   A. 1,350   B. 2,700   C. 5,400   D. 10,800

21. The active (oxidized) form of hematoxylin that binds color to tissues is

   A. hematin   B. hemosiderin
   C. hematein   D. hematoidin

22. The FUNDAMENTAL role played by mordants in certain staining procedures depends upon the ability of these substances to 22.____

    A. bind dyes to tissues
    B. alter color properties of dyes
    C. shorten time needed for dyes to stain tissues
    D. prolong the shelf life of dyes

23. The CHIEF advantage of the rotary microtome over the sliding microtome is that it 23.____

    A. cuts ribbons of sections
    B. is easier to operate
    C. costs less
    D. cuts both celloidin and paraffin blocks

24. An IMPORTANT chemical reagent used in the preparation of both Benin's and Zenker's fixing fluids is 24.____

    A. picric acid   B. acetic acid
    C. mercuric chloride   D. sodium sulfate

25. A tissue component NOT stained by the periodic acid-Schiff procedure (PAS negative) is 25.____

    A. liver glycogen   B. intercellular matrix of cartilage
    C. basement membranes   D. chromosomes

26. In working up tissue sections fixed in Zenker's or Kelly's fluid, an alcoholic iodine solution is employed and followed by sodium thiosulphate in order to remove 26.____

    A. vanadium crystals   B. mercury deposits
    C. bismuth compounds   D. insoluble amyloid

27. Pyknosis is a term used to describe nuclei that are _____ and _____ . 27.____

    A. swollen; hyperchromatic   B. swollen; hypochromatic
    C. shrunken; hyperchromatic   D. shrunken; hypochromatic

28. A stratified squamous epithelium is a multilayered cellular covering in which _____ are squamous. 28.____

    A. all of the cells are
    B. only the cells on the superficial surface
    C. only the cells in the basal layer
    D. only the intermediate layers of cells

29. The ability of certain tissues to take on color tints that are different from the characteristic color of the dye used is referred to as 29.____

    A. metachromasia   B. polychromasia
    C. allochromasia   D. orthochromasia

30. As a group, exocrine glands are aggregates of secretory epithelial cells which pass their secretions into 30.____

    A. arteries   B. veins
    C. lymphatic channels   D. ducts

KEY (CORRECT ANSWERS)

1. D
2. B
3. D
4. B
5. C

6. C
7. D
8. C
9. B
10. A

11. A
12. B
13. D
14. C
15. B

16. C
17. D
18. C
19. B
20. B

21. C
22. A
23. A
24. B
25. D

26. B
27. C
28. B
29. A
30. D

TEST 3

DIRECTIONS: Each question or incomplete statement is followed by several suggested answers or completions. Select the one that BEST answers the question or completes the statement. *PRINT THE LETTER OF THE CORRECT ANSWER IN THE SPACE AT THE RIGHT.*

Questions 1-15. **MICROBIOLOGY**

DIRECTIONS: Questions 1 through 15 are to be answered on the basis of microbiology.

1. After the addition of alcohol during the process of preparing a Gram stain, the Gram-negative cell becomes

   A. blue B. pink C. brown D. colorless

2. Which of the following Gram negative bacteria would BEST be isolated on an alkaline medium (pH 8.4)?

   A. Vibrio comma
   B. Escherichia coli
   C. Neisseria gonorrhea
   D. Citrobacter freundii

3. The medium used in antibiotic sensitivity testing by the Kirby-Bauer method is _____ agar.

   A. Mueller-Hinton
   B. Brain-heart infusion
   C. trypticase soy
   D. thioglycollate

4. Serum tellurite agar medium is used for the isolation of pathogenic members of the genus

   A. Streptococcus
   B. Pseudomonas
   C. Corynebacteria
   D. Salmonella

5. A yeast-like organism that is EASILY identified by its large capsule is

   A. Histoplasma capsulatum
   B. Cryptococcus neoformans
   C. Sporotrichum schenckii
   D. Biastomyces dermatiditis

6. The MOST effective method of sterilization of bacteriological media is to

   A. heat in a hot air oven at 160°C for 30 minutes
   B. boil the media for 30 minutes
   C. autoclave at 121°C for 20 minutes
   D. autoclave at 115°C for 20 minutes

7. ALL pathogenic bacteria can be classed as

   A. aerobes
   B. anaerobes
   C. psychrotrophs
   D. mesotrophs

8. Which of the following pathogenic organisms can be grown on blood agar?

   A. Salmonella typhi, Rabies virus, and Streptococcus pyogenes
   B. Staphylococcus aureus, Pseudomonas aeruginosa, and Mycobacterium leprae
   C. Neisseria meningitidis, Salmonella typhi, and Staph-ylococcus aureus
   D. Diplococcus pneumoniae, Influenza virus, and Hemo-philus influenzae

9. Complete lysis of erythrocytes in the Wasserman test indicates that a patient

   A. has syphilis
   B. does not have syphilis
   C. has gonorrhea
   D. does not have gonorrhea

10. The MOST definite test for pathogenic Staphylococci is

    A. hemolysis of erythrocytes
    B. mannitol fermentation
    C. tellurite reduction
    D. production of coagulase

11. Which one of the following would be a satisfactory enrichment medium for a suspected Salmonella-infected stool specimen?

    A. Blood agar
    B. EMB plate
    C. Selenite broth
    D. MacConkey agar

12. Growths of Diplococcus pneumoniae and Streptococcus fecalis on blood agar plates can closely resemble one another.
    The MORE pathogenic organism may be identified by

    A. a positive Quellung reaction
    B. its ability to grow in SF medium
    C. a high anti-streptolysin O titer
    D. a low anti-streptolysin O titer

13. Two media that can be used for the primary isolation of Neisseria gonorrhea are

    A. Mueller-Hinton agar and trypticase soy agar
    B. chocolate agar and Thayer-Martin agar
    C. trypticase soy agar and blood agar
    D. chocolate agar and trypticase soy agar

14. Pathogenic members of the Enterobacteriaceae USUALLY will

    A. produce H_2S on a TSI slant
    B. produce gas from glucose
    C. not ferment lactose
    D. exhibit motility

15. A test that differentiates Salmonella from Proteus is the

    A. urease test
    B. motility test
    C. production of hydrogen sulfide
    D. fermentation of lactose

Questions 16-30.   **TOXICOLOGY**

DIRECTIONS: Questions 16 through 30 are to be answered on the basis of toxicology.

16. Assume that you are required to determine lead in body tissue or fluid. Which one of the following instrumental methods should you use?

    A. Infrared spectroscopy
    B. Ultraviolet spectroscopy
    C. Atomic absorption
    D. Nuclear magnetic resonance spectrometry

17. What is the pH of the commonly used buffer, phosphate buffered saline?

    A. 6.5   B. 7.4   C. 8.3   D. 9.2

18. What is the MOST important component of a pH meter?

    A. Water   B. Hydrochloric acid
    C. Electrode   D. Standard buffer

19. What is the MOST rapid method for qualitatively assaying for drugs of abuse from human body tissue or fluid?

    A. Gas chromatography
    B. Atomic absorption
    C. Thin layer chromatography
    D. Mass spectrometry

20. The CORRECT chemical structure for bis (?-chloromethyl) ether is

    A. $ClCH_2 \; O \; CH_2 \; Cl$
    B. $Cl_2CH \; O \; CH_3$
    C. $ClCH_2CH_2O \; CH_2Cl$
    D. $ClCH_2CH_2OCH_2CH_2Cl$

21. The APPROXIMATE spectrophotometric range of an ultraviolet-visible spectrophotometer is

    A. 250-2000 nm   B. 200-750 nm
    C. 100-300 nm   D. 3000-1200 cm^{-1}

22. Which one of the following elements occurs as salts ONLY in bivalent form?

    A. Phosphorus   B. Sodium
    C. Calcium   D. Mercury

23. Which one of the following instruments gives BOTH excitation and emission spectra?

    A. Ultraviolet spectrophotometer
    B. Fluorescence spectrophotometer
    C. Mass spectrometer
    D. NMR spectrometer

24. Sulfuric acid gives a white precipitate with water-soluble salts of which one of the following?

    A. Sodium   B. Barium   C. Ammonia   D. Magnesium

25. For what purpose is azeotropic distillation used?

    A. Removal of water   B. Lyophilization
    C. Sublimation   D. Vacuum distillation

26. Which one of the following materials is transparent to infrared irradiation?

    A. Potassium bromide   B. Benzene
    C. Cyclohexane   D. Chloroform

27. The NORMAL pathlength for an ultraviolet quartz cell is

    A. 0.1 inch   B. 1 cm   C. 1.0 inch   D. 10 cm

28. Assume that you are analyzing for a mixture of traces of chlorinated hydrocarbon pesticides.
    Which one of the following instruments should you use?

    A. Infrared   B. Gas chromatography
    C. Atomic absorption   D. Ultraviolet spectroscopy

29. The SMALLEST amount of a pure material that can be conveniently analyzed for by infrared spectroscopy is

    A. 5 micrograms   B. 1 ing
    C. 10 milligrams   D. 1 gram

30. Ethylene diamine tetraacetic acid is MOST commonly used as a

    A. chelating agent   B. solvent
    C. buffer   D. detergent

KEY (CORRECT ANSWERS)

1.	D	16.	C
2.	A	17.	B
3.	A	18.	C
4.	C	19.	C
5.	B	20.	A
6.	C	21.	B
7.	D	22.	C
8.	C	23.	B
9.	B	24.	B
10.	D	25.	A
11.	C	26.	A
12.	A	27.	B
13.	B	28.	B
14.	C	29.	A
15.	A	30.	A

BASIC FUNDAMENTALS OF MEDICATION ADMINISTRATION

CONTENTS

	Page
I. GUIDELINES FOR MEDICATION ADMINISTRATION	1
A. General	1
B. Unit Dose	3
II. MEDICATION ADMINISTRATION RECORD	4
III. DROPS	7
A. Ear	7
B. Eye	8
C. Nose	9
IV. GASTRIC TUBES	10
V. HEPARIN LOCKS	11
VI. INJECTIONS	12
A. General	12
B. Intramuscular	14
1. Z-Tract	15
C. Intradermal	15
D. Intravenous Piggyback	16
E. Subcutaneous	18
1. Insulin	18
VII. ORAL MEDICATIONS	19
A. Tablets, Pills, or Capsules	20
B. Powders	20
C. Liquids	20
VIII. SUPPOSITORIES	21
A. Rectal	21
B. Urethral	22
C. Vaginal	23

BASIC FUNDAMENTALS OF MEDICATION ADMINISTRATION

I. GUIDELINES FOR MEDICATION ADMINISTRATION

A. General

PURPOSE

To administer the <u>right medication</u>, in the <u>right dose</u>, by the <u>right route</u>, to the <u>right patient</u>, at the <u>right time</u>

PROCEDURE	SPECIAL CONSIDERATIONS

• Transcribe medication and treatment orders from doctor's orders to
    • Medication and Treatment Cards
    • Nursing Care Plan
    • Medication Administration Record (MAR)
	Follow local policy.

• Check ALL Medication and Treatment Cards against Nursing Care Plan at the beginning of each shift.	
• Return cards to medication and treatment board, placing each card in space corresponding to hour when medication is due. • Clean working area.	
• Wash your hands.	
• Obtain supplies and equipment such as tongue blades, paper cups, pitcher of water, medication tray or cart, and stethoscope.	Keep cards for same patient together.

• Separate cards into
    • oral medications
    • injections
    • treatments	

• Arrange cards in sequence similar to placement of patients on ward.	
• Turn cards face down, turn top card up, and read information on card.	
• Locate medication and compare label on medication with name of medication and dosage on card.	FIRST MEDICATION CHECK.

GUIDELINES FOR MEDICATION ADMINISTRATION, GENERAL (cont)

PROCEDURE	SPECIAL CONSIDERATIONS
• Remove medication container and compare label on container with name of medication and dosage on card.	SECOND CHECK.
• Pour required dosage and compare label on container with card for name of medication and dosage.	THIRD CHECK.
• Place medication and card on tray or cart.	NEVER leave medication cart or tray unattended.
• Continue with remaining cards in same manner.	
• Lock medication cabinet before leaving the area.	
• Administer only medications that you personally prepared.	NEVER allow others to administer medication that you prepared.
• Check name on bed tag with name on card.	FIRST ID CHECK.
• Compare name on card with patient's ID band.	SECOND CHECK.
• Ask patient: "What is your name?" Be sure response is accurate.	THIRD CHECK.
• Administer medication ONLY if all 3 checks agree.	
• Place card face down on one side of tray.	
• Continue to administer medications until all are given.	
• Reset tray or cart for next use.	
• Take cards to desk.	
• Record medications, time and date given, and your initials on MAR using cards as guide.	
• Replace cards on board at next hour due.	

B. *Unit Dose*

PURPOSE

To administer single-dose medication in ready-to-use form

PROCEDURE	SPECIAL CONSIDERATIONS
• See "Guidelines for Medication Administration, General."	
• Get stocked medication cart from storage area.	Cart is stocked by pharmacy personnel.
• Unlock cart.	
• Wheel medication cart to bedside, check MAR, and identify patient.	Follow local policy.

• Open cassette drawer.
  • Read MAR.
  • Select medication from cassette drawer.	

• Check medication against MAR for date, dosage, and route.	

• Administer medication and record immediately on MAR.
  • Remain with patient until medication has been taken.
  • Replace drawer in correct space in cassette.	

• Dispose of litter, syringe, and needle before moving to next patient.
  • Break off tip of needle and syringe, and dispose in dirty needle box.
  • Place glass unit dose liquid container in bag for return to pharmacy.	

• Lock cart and return to storage area.	

II. MEDICATION ADMINISTRATION RECORD (MAR)

PURPOSE
To maintain a permanent record of medication administered

PROCEDURE	SPECIAL CONSIDERATIONS
• Stamp MAR with Addressograph as shown in figure 6-1 on the following page.	
• Enter ward number at bottom right of form; record month and year in space provided at the top.	Make all entries in black ink.
• Transcribe scheduled medications from doctor's orders to front of form.	
• Enter order date, medication dosage, frequency, and route of administration.	
• Complete "Hours" column to indicate scheduled hours for administration starting with earliest military time after 2400 hours.	
• Complete "Dates Given" blocks at top of form.	
• Enter month and dates for a 7 day period, starting with first day medication is given.	
• Cancel vacant spaces with an "X."	
• Draw a heavy line across page under last entry and enter next medication directly below.	Do not skip a space.
• When medication has been given, enter your initials in column corresponding to date and hour of administration.	
• Place an "*" in column if the medication was not given and state reason on Nursing Notes.	
• Place an "L" under date and opposite hour patient is on liberty.	Follow local policy.
• When medication is stopped, bracket remaining spaces for that day; write "STOPPED," enter date and initials.	Applies to scheduled drugs, PRN, and variable dose medications.
• Complete "Initial Code" section.	

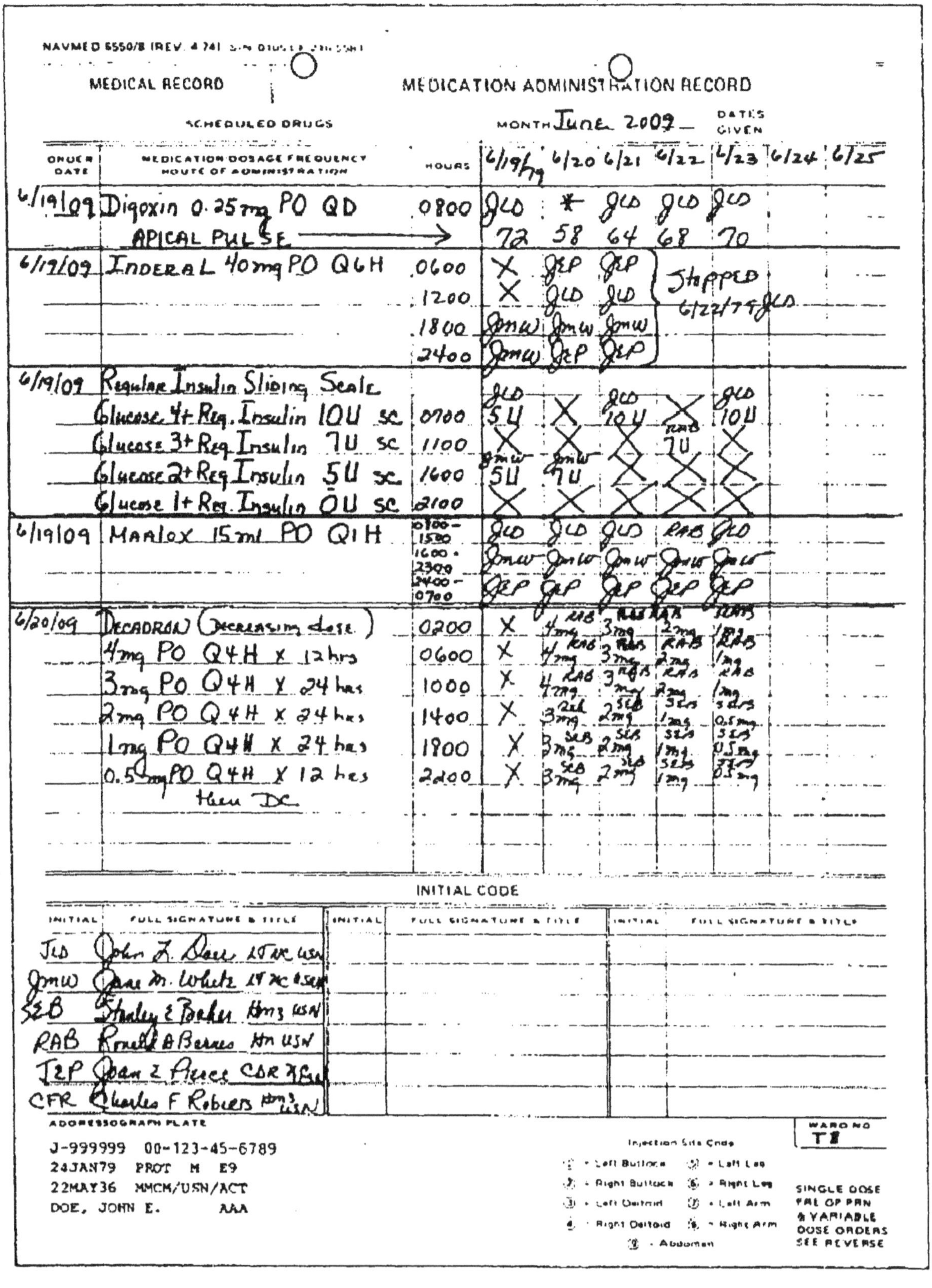

Figure 1. Sample Entries on Medication Administration Record (Front).

MEDICATION ADMINISTRATION RECORD (cont)

PROCEDURE	SPECIAL CONSIDERATIONS
• Transcribe single-order medication, dosage, route of administration, and date and time to be given on back of form. See figure 2 on the following page.	
• After administering medication, initial appropriate block.	
• Transcribe each preoperative (PREOP) medication dosage, and route of administration on succeeding lines.	A bracket may be used to show that all PREOP medications are to be given on the same date and time.
• Enter your initials after administering medications.	
• Transcribe PRN and variable dose medications from doctor's orders to back of form (fig. 2).	
• Enter order date, medication, dosage, frequency, route, and reason for medication.	For variable dose medications, the dosage need not be the same for each entry.
• Enter date, time, dose, and your initials after administering medication.	

NOTE: Some medication orders require modification of basic transcription and charting techniques (fig. 1). These include:

  • increasing or decreasing dose medications
  • medications requiring apical pulse assessment before administration
  • medications administered every other day
  • medications such as insulin administered per sliding scale

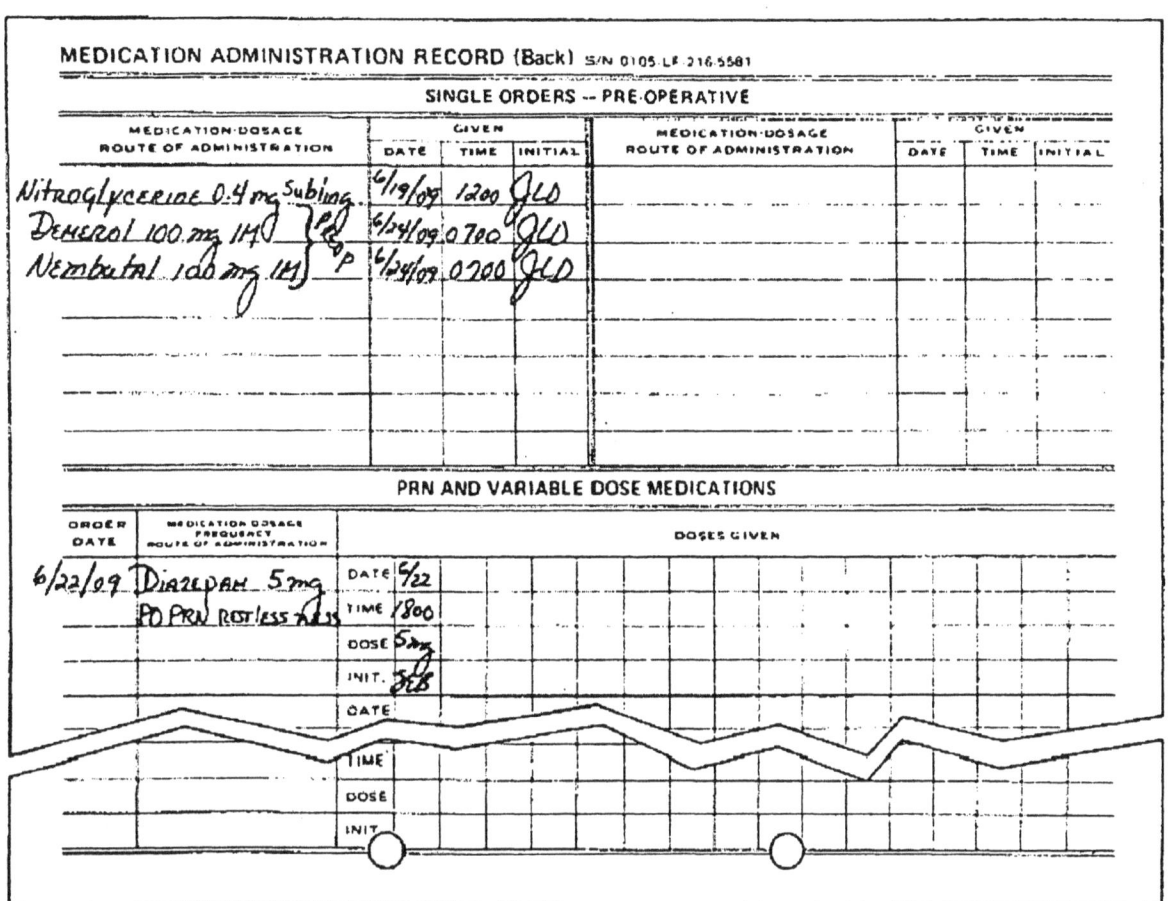

Figure 2. Sample Entries on Medication Administration Record (Back).

III. DROPS
A. Ear

PURPOSE
To instill medication into the auditory canal

PROCEDURE	SPECIAL CONSIDERATIONS
• See "Guidelines for Medication Administration, General."	Patients should have their own properly labeled medication and it should be at room temperature.
• Position patient on side with affected ear upward.	
• Clean external auditory canal gently with cotton applicators.	Avoid traumatizing when dry-wiping ear canal.
• Straighten auditory canal by gently pulling lobe upward and backward.	

DROPS, EAR (cont)

PROCEDURE

- Instill prescribed number of drops holding dropper nearly horizontally.

- Place cotton loosely in external auditory canal (if ordered).

- Instruct patient to remain in position with treated ear upward for about 5 minutes.

SPECIAL CONSIDERATIONS

Support head as needed. Allow medication to fall to side of canal.

SUPPLIES AND EQUIPMENT

Applicators, cotton tipped   Cotton balls

B. Eye
(Ointment Included)

PURPOSE
To apply medication to eye tissue

PROCEDURE

- See "Guidelines for Medication Administration."

- Verify eye to be medicated.

- Tilt patient's head backward and sideways so solution will run away from tear duct.

- Clean eye gently with cotton ball.

- Retract lower lid.

- Instruct patient to look upward.

- Drop medication onto lower lid as shown in figure 3.

SPECIAL CONSIDERATIONS

If both drops and ointment are ordered, instill drops before applying ointment. Patients should have their own properly labeled medication.
Some solutions are toxic if absorbed through the nose or pharynx.

Do not permit dropper or tip of ointment tube to touch the eye. Avoid contaminating medicine container.

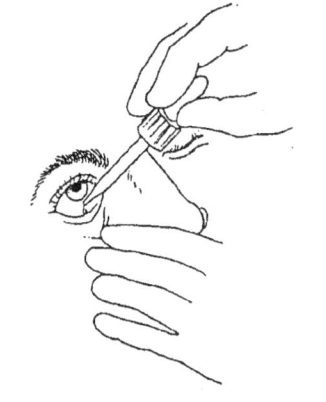

Figure 3. Instilling Eye Drops.

DROPS, EYE (cont)
PROCEDURE
- Apply ointment onto conjunctiva of lower lid as illustrated in figure 4.

- Place dropper in bottle or put cap on ointment tube.

- Instruct patient to close eye.

- Wipe excess medication from inner to outer eye with sterile 2x2s then discard.

SPECIAL CONSIDERATIONS

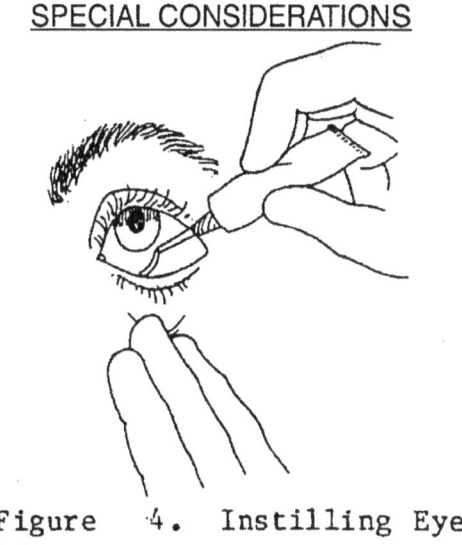

Figure 4. Instilling Eye Ointment.

SUPPLIES AND EQUIPMENT
Cotton balls   Sterile gauze 2x2s

c. Nose

PURPOSE
- To instill medication into the nose

PROCEDURE
- See "Guidelines for Medication Administration."

- Tilt patient's head backwards.

- Fill dropper with medication.

- Instill prescribed dosage into nostril as shown in figure 5.

- Place tissues within easy reach.

- Keep patient in position for about 2 minutes.

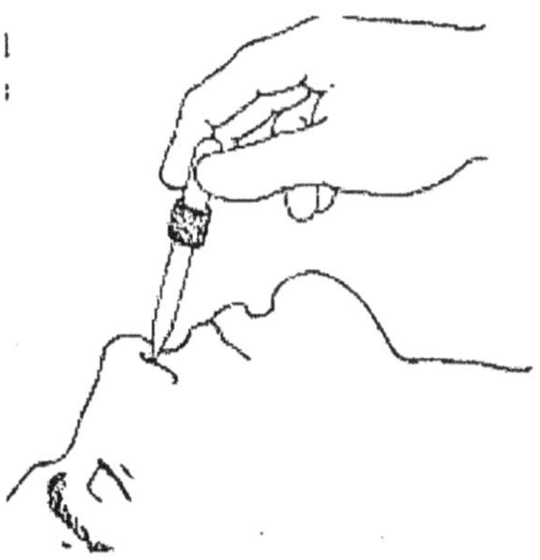

Figure 5. Instilling Nose Drops.

SPECIAL CONSIDERATIONS

Patients should have their own properly labeled medication.

Do not permit medication to touch rubber bulb of dropper.

Avoid touching nostril with tip of dropper.

IV. GASTRIC TUBES

PURPOSE
To administer medications into the stomach through a tube

PROCEDURE	SPECIAL CONSIDERATIONS
• See "Guidelines for Medication Administration, General."	
• Crush all tablets and add 30 ml tap water.	
• Assemble equipment and take to bedside.	
• Elevate head of bed unless contraindicated.	Decreases risk of aspiration and regurgitation.
• Expose feeding tube.	
• Place protective pad under tubes.	
• Check stomach tube for correct placement. • Aspirate for gastric contents. • Listen with stethoscope for air entering stomach as 5 to 10 cc of air is injected into tube.	Notify physician if tube is not placed properly.
• Attach irrigating syringe to tube with plunger removed.	
• Instill medication into irrigating syringe.	
• Follow medication with 30 ml water and allow to flow by gravity.	Ensures patient receives all medication.
• Clamp tube and cover end for 20 to 30 minutes unless contraindicated.	Allows medicine to be absorbed.
• Reattach tube to suction if indicated.	
• Rinse and clean;syringe with tap water.	
• Return syringe to bedside storage.	
• Record amount of water instilled on I&O worksheet.	
• Record medication administered on MAR.	

GASTRIC TUBES (cont)

Clamp Emesis basin Gauze sponges 4x4

SUPPLIES AND EQUIPMENT

Irrigating syringe, 60 ml Protective pad Rubber band

Sterile dressing (if ordered) Stethoscope Tap water

V. HEPARIN LOCKS

PURPOSE

To administer medications through a heparin lock

PROCEDURE

- See "Guidelines for Medication Administration, General."

- Assemble IV piggyback (IVPB) medication and IV administration set; attach small gauge needle to end of tubing.

- Fill two 2 1/2 ml syringes with 2 ml normal saline.

- Withdraw 0.9 ml normal saline and 0.1 ml heparin 1:1000 into a TB syringe.

- Take equipment to bedside.

- Determine patency of heparin lock.
  - Attach first 2 1/2 ml syringe with saline.
  - Aspirate and observe for blood return.
  - If no blood returns, check for infiltration by slowly injecting small amount of normal saline.
  - If infiltrated, remove heparin lock and insert new one.

- Flush lock with 2 ml normal saline to flush out heparin.

- Attach IVPB medication infusion set to heparin lock.

- Administer medication.

- Flush lock with second syringe of normal saline.

SPECIAL CONSIDERATIONS

Incompatibilities may exist resulting in a precipitate.

HEPARIN LOCKS (cont)

PROCEDURE

SPECIAL CONSIDERATIONS

- Flush lock with heparin solution.

- Record medication given on MAR.

SUPPLIES AND EQUIPMENT

Alcohol sponges Heparin 1:1000	IV administration set IVPB infusion set Needle, 23 ga	Syringes, 2 1/2 ml (2), TB (1)

IV. INJECTIONS

A. *General*

In this section, intramuscular, intradermal, and subcutaneous injections are outlined. Many of the steps are the same for all three methods of injection. Therefore, follow the basic procedure listed below and refer to the specific procedure for special details and equipment.

PROCEDURE

SPECIAL CONSIDERATIONS

- See "Guidelines for Medication Administration, General."

See equipment list of specific procedure.

- Assemble equipment in preparation area.
  - Remove syringe from sterile pack.
  - Loosen the plunger by withdrawing once or twice.
- Assemble syringe and needle.

- Tighten needle.

- Score ampule with file if not prescored.

Prescored ampules are usually indicated by colored ring.

- Clean ampule or vial with antiseptic sponge and break away top of ampule.

- Discard ampule top and sponge.

- Remove needle guard and place on counter for reuse.

- Draw enough air into syringe to equal in volume the dose of medication ordered.

Does not apply to ampules.

INJECTIONS, GENERAL (cont)

PROCEDURE

• Insert needle into medication using aseptic technique. See figure 6.

• Withdraw slightly more medication than required dose.

• Remove needle from ampule or vial.

• Hold syringe and needle vertically.
  • Tap syringe with finger to dislodge air bubbles.
  • Aspirate to clear needle of solution.
  • Push solution up to needle hub.
  • Tip needle and syringe expelling excess solution into sink.
  • Cover and remove used needle.
  • Attach new sterile needle.
  • Read calibrations on syringe barrel at eye level to ensure correct dosage.

• Take syringe and antiseptic sponge to patient's bedside.

• Identify patient.

• Explain procedure to patient.

• Select injection site and position patient accordingly, avoiding undue exposure.

• Clean area with antiseptic sponge.

SPECIAL CONSIDERATIONS

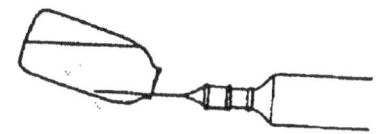

Figure 6. Withdrawing Medication from Ampule.

Do not allow solution to run down shaft of needle.

REFER TO SPECIFIC PROCEDURE: INTRAMUSCULAR, Z-TRACT, INTRADERMAL, INTRAVE-NOUS, SUBCUTANEOUS, OR INSULIN. After performing specific procedure

• Clip off needle and tip of syringe then discard.

B. *Intramuscular*
(IM)

PURPOSE

To administer <u>sterile</u> medications intramuscularly

PROCEDURE

- See "Injections, General."

- Select injection site. See figure 7.

- Position patient.
    - Place on abdomen "toeing in" for gluteal area.
    - Place on side for ventral gluteal area.

- Clean area with antiseptic sponge.

- Hold tissue taut and insert needle at 90° angle as shown in figure 8.

- Aspirate. If blood appears
    - withdraw needle
    - discard medication
    - prepare new dose
- Inject medication slowly.

- Remove needle quickly while holding skin taut.

- Place antiseptic sponge over injection site exerting slight pressure.

SPECIAL CONSIDERATIONS

Preferred site is the ventral gluteal area.

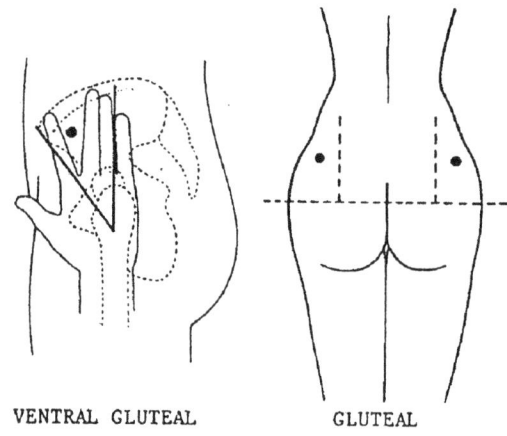

Figure 7. Intramuscular Injection Sites.

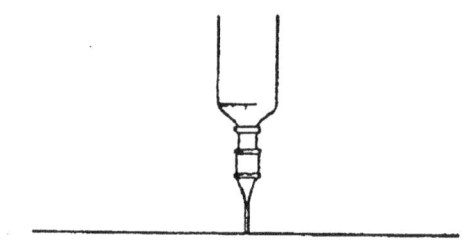

Figure 8. Intramuscular Injection Angle.

SUPPLIES AND EQUIPMENT

| Antiseptic sponges (2) | Syringe, 1 to 5 ml | Needle, 21 or 22 ga, 1 1/4 ga |

1. Z-Tract

PURPOSE
To prevent backflow of medication from IM injection into subcutaneous tissue

PROCEDURE
- See "Injections, General."

- Position patient.

  - Place on abdomen "toeing in" for gluteal area.
    - Place on back for vastus lateralis area.
    - Place on side for ventral gluteal area.

- Clean area with antiseptic sponge.

- Pull skin downward or to the side and insert the needle proximal to midmuscle mass downward at an oblique angle.

- Insert needle quickly with bevel up.

- Aspirate. If blood appears
  - withdraw needle
  - discard medication
  - prepare new dose

- Inject medication slowly and empty syringe completely.

- Remove needle quickly, holding skin taut.

- Release skin and wipe area with antiseptic sponge.

SPECIAL CONSIDERATIONS

C. *Intradermal* (ID)

PURPOSE
To test for sensitivity to foreign substances

PROCEDURE
- See "Injections, General."

- Select injection site.

- Clean area with antiseptic sponge.

SPECIAL CONSIDERATIONS
Usual dose for ID testing is 0.1 ml or less.

INJECTIONS, ID (cont)

PROCEDURE
• Grasp forearm securely on both sides of injection site.
　• Place thumb on one side and forefinger on the other.
　• Hold skin taut.

• Insert needle just under skin surface at a 15° angle with bevel up. See figure 9.

• Inject solution slowly to produce a bubble or wheal.

• Remove needle.

• Read skin test.

SPECIAL CONSIDERATIONS

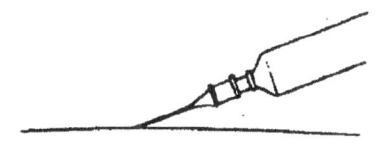

Figure 9. Intradermal Injection Angle.

Do not massage.

Follow local policy.

SUPPLIES AND EQUIPMENT

Antiseptic sponges (2)　　Needle, 26 or 27 ga, 1 in　　Syringe, TB

D. *Intravenous Piggyback*
(IVPB)

PURPOSE
　To administer medications through an IV line

PROCEDURE
　• See "Guidelines for Medication Administration, General."

　• Units with IV admixture

　　• Check for correctness of medication as in guidelines above.

　• Units without IV admixture

　　• Prepare medications and draw into syringe.
　　• Obtain secondary IV solution ensuring compatibility with medication.
　　• Inject medication into secondary IV solution.
　　　• Label solution with
　　　　• name of medication
　　　　• dosage
　　　　• date
　　　　• time
　　　　• your initials

SPECIAL CONSIDERATIONS

Pharmacy may prepare fluids with added medications.

Do not cover manufacturer's label.

INJECTIONS, IVPB (cont)
PROCEDURE

- Close regulator clamp on IVPB administration set.

- Insert piercing pin through stopper.

- Attach needle to tubing.

- Clear air from tubing and needle.

- Label tubing with
  - date
  - time
  - your initials

- Take equipment to bedside.

- Identify patient as in guidelines above.

- Have secondary IV on standard.
- Clean upper Y-junction on primary IV set with alcohol swab.

- Insert secondary needle into Y.

- Secure needle with tape.

- Open clamp on secondary set and adjust rate.

- Record amount of fluid infused on I&O worksheet.

- Record medication on MAR.

SPECIAL CONSIDERATIONS

Maintain aseptic technique.

Local policy dictates size of needle.

Tubing and needle must be changed every 24 hours.

Primary and secondary IVs. run simultaneously. IVPBs may not run unless primary bottle is lower. It is not necessary to adjust flow rate of primary bottle. It will begin again when IVPB is empty.

SUPPLIES AND EQUIPMENT

Adhesive tape	IV administration set	Label
Alcohol swabs	IV solution (50 to 150 ml)	Needle, 23 to 19 ga

E. *Subcutaneous*
(SC)

PURPOSE
To administer medications subcutaneously

PROCEDURE
- See "Injections, General."

- Select injection site. See figure 10.

- Clean area with antiseptic sponge.

- Pinch skin between thumb and forefinger.

- Insert needle at 45° angle with bevel up as shown in figure 11.

- Aspirate. If blood appears
  - withdraw needle
  - discard medication
  - prepare new dose
- Inject medication slowly.

- Withdraw needle quickly.

- Place antiseptic sponge over site and apply gentle pressure.

SPECIAL CONSIDERATIONS

Another acceptable site is the anterior lateral aspect of the thigh.

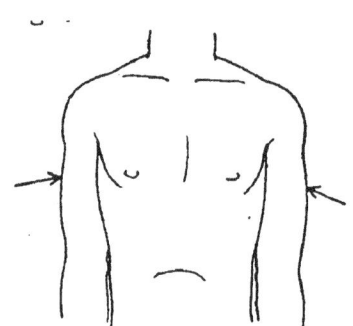

Figure 10. Subcutaneous Injection Site.

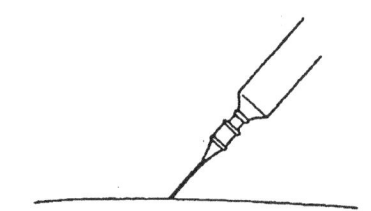

Figure 11. Subcutaneous Injection Angle.

SUPPLIES AND EQUIPMENT
Antiseptic sponges (2) Needle, 23 ga, 3/4 in Syringe, 2 1/2 ml

1. Insulin

PURPOSE
To lower blood sugar

PROCEDURE

- See "Injections, General."

- Roll insulin vial between palms to thoroughly mix and warm.

SPECIAL CONSIDERATIONS

INJECTIONS, SC, Insulin (cont)
PROCEDURE
• Have another person (nurse) check dose you prepare.

• Select injection site. See figure 12.
  • Rotate injection sites systematically as directed by local policy.

• Clean area with antiseptic sponge.

• Pinch skin between thumb and forefinger.

• Insert needle at 45° angle with bevel up (fig. ID.

• Aspirate. If blood appears
  • withdraw needle
  • discard medication
  • prepare new dose

• Inject medication slowly.

• Withdraw needle quickly.

• Place antiseptic sponge over site and apply gentle pressure.

SPECIAL CONSIDERATIONS

Do not give to an NPO patient without consulting physician for specific instructions.

Absorption from the arm is more rapid than from the thigh

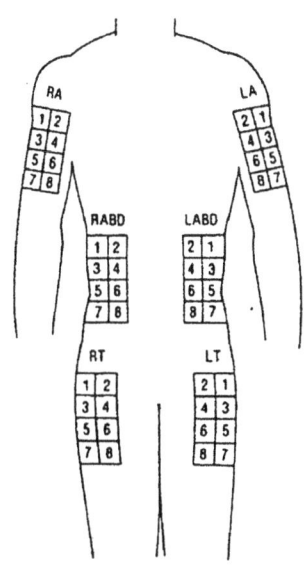

Figure 12. Insulin Injection Sites.

Needle, 23 ga, 3/4 in

SUPPLIES AND EQUIPMENT
Syringe, insulin

VII. ORAL MEDICATIONS

PURPOSE
To prepare and administer medications orally

PROCEDURE

• See "Guidelines for Medication Administration, General."

SPECIAL CONSIDERATIONS

ORAL MEDICATIONS (cont)

PROCEDURE	SPECIAL CONSIDERATIONS
A. Tablets, Pills, or Capsules	
• Instruct patient how to take medication.	For example, if medication is given sublingually, let pill dissolve under toague.

• Check apical pulse rate for 1 full minute before giving cardiotonics.
   Do not give if rate is below 60 per minute.
    • Notify nurse or physician.
    • Record on MAR.	

B. Powders	
• Remove powdered medications from container with a clean, dry, tongue depressor.	
C. Liquids	
• Shake medication if it is a precipitate.	
• Remove bottle, cap and place on counter inside up.	
• Hold bottle with label covered by your palm to prevent soiling label.	
• Measure liquids at eye level using calibrated medication cup.	
• Wipe rim of bottle before recapping.	
• If medication is ordered in drops, count them aloud.	

• Dilute irons, acids, and iodides in 120 ml water and have patient drink through straw.
    • Irons and iodides stain teeth.
    • Acids and iodides can irritate mouth.	

• Give cough medications after all others are taken.	Do not dilute or give water following liquid cough medications.

VIII. SUPPOSITORIES
A. Rectal

PURPOSE
To administer medication rectally

PROCEDURE

- See "Guidelines for Medication Administration, General."

- Screen patient.

- Place patient in left Sim's position.

- Remove protective wrapper from medication.

- Don finger cot or disposable glove.

- Separate buttocks.

- Insert suppository gently through anal opening about 2 inches, using index finger.

- Have patient try to retain suppository for 20 minutes if given to cause bowel movement.

- Hold buttocks together for a minute or two to ensure absorption.

- Remove glove or finger cot and discard.

- Wash your hands.

- Assist patient to a comfortable position as needed.

SPECIAL CONSIDERATIONS

Others can be retained indefinitely.

SUPPLIES AND EQUIPMENT

Finger cot or glove

B. *Urethral*

PURPOSE

To administer medication through the urethra

PROCEDURE

• See "Guidelines for Medication Administration, General."

• Screen patient.

Females

• Place patient on back, legs drawn up and apart, with perineum exposed.

• Remove suppository from wrapper.

• Don disposable glove.

• Separate labia with thumb and forefinger and insert suppository. See figure 13.

• Remove glove and discard.

• Wash your hands.

Males

• Place patient on back with perineum exposed.

• Remove suppository from wrapper.

• Don disposable glove.

• Grasp penis with thumb and forefinger of one hand to expose meatus.

• Insert suppository.

• Remove glove and discard.

• Wash your hands.

Glove, disposable

SPECIAL CONSIDERATIONS

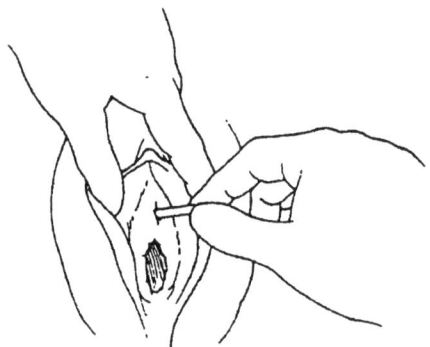

Figure 13. Inserting a Urethral Suppository.

Replace foreskin in uncircum-cised males to prevent constriction.

SUPPLIES AND EQUIPMENT

c. Vaginal

PURPOSE
To administer medication vaginally

PROCEDURE,

- See "Guidelines for Medication Administration, General."

- Screen patient.

- Position patient in dorsal lithotomy position and expose perineum.

- Remove suppository from wrapper.

- Don disposable glove.

- Separate labia with thumb and forefinger.

- Insert suppository about 2 inches upward and backward into vagina.

- Remove glove and discard.

- Assist patient to comfortable position as needed.

- Wash your hands.

SPECIAL CONSIDERATIONS

SUPPLIES AND EQUIPMENT

Finger cot or glove

www.ingramcontent.com/pod-product-compliance
Lightning Source LLC
Chambersburg PA
CBHW081831300426
44116CB00014B/2550